DICK FOR A DAY

Dick for a Day

*What Would You Do
If You Had One?*

EDITED BY FIONA GILES

Villard   New York

FRONTISPIECE:"Cherry Girl," by Amy Jenkins

Library of Congress Cataloging-in-Publication Data
Dick for a day / edited by Fiona Giles.
p.   cm.
ISBN 0-679-77353-3
1. Penis—Humor.   2. Penis—Social aspects.   3. Women—Sexual
behavior.   I. Giles, Fiona.
PN6231.P344D53   1997
810.8'03538—dc20   96-34868

To my Dick

ACKNOWLEDGMENTS

It is impossible to name everyone who has helped with suggestions, contacts, and encouragement, but special thanks are due to Janice Eidus, Yael Kanarek, Matthew Martin, Ken Wark, Inez Baranay, Rachel Knepfer, Belinda Luscombe, Bernard Cohen, Janyce Stefan-Cole, Amruta Slee, and Lily Brett, all of whom gave freely of their ideas, goodwill, and expertise. My thanks, also, to all the contributors for their wonderful stories, poems, essays, artwork, and quotations; to Elaine Markson and Pari Berk at Elaine Markson and Associates, for their unsurpassed practical and emotional support; to David Rosenthal and everyone at Villard Books, for being creative enough to launch my vision; and to my husband, Richard Andrews, for helping me, in every way, to get it up.

CONTENTS

x 🛉 **Contents**

Introduction

FIONA GILES

Loved, hated, played with—discussed and disgusting, adored and reviled—the penis inspires controversy and ambivalence as much as it represents the possibility of new life, the best of procreative value, and the worst of patriarchal excess. It can be the magic wand that bestows pleasure and love—or the brutal or indifferent instrument of abuse and pain; women's experience of the penis ranges from the sublime to the ridiculous, from the transcendent to the mundane.

But what if a woman could try one out, just for a day? To what uses might it be put? What mischief and adventures, or simple opportunities to inhabit new space? What object lessons for its everyday owners, the men we love?

In this collection, a number of women writers, poets, and artists put their minds to answering the question, What would you like to do if, by some mysterious means, you had a penis for one day? The point is not to promote the myth of penis envy; obviously, women don't need a penis, and most likely very few would want one as a permanent fixture, especially if it meant giving up what they already possess. But entertaining the idea, if ever so briefly, this book reveals what women really think of the phallus as both anatomical object and cultural archetype: its potential to please when put in expert hands, to transform when driven by the fresh perspectives of its consumers—its fans, its victims, its mistresses.

Dick for a Day allows a wide variety of women writers and artists (together with two men) to develop fantasies of appropriation; it gives them a chance to hijack maleness in whatever form they choose, from one-liners, cartoons, and poetry to short stories and essays. The book casts a wide net over female perspectives on the penis, ranging outside the better-explored lesbian use of masculine indicators. While also including lesbian and bisexual writers, *Dick for a Day* is particularly interested in what a heterosexual woman would make of a penis if one sprouted from her body, or if—as a number of writers preferred—she received one in the mail. Rather than focus on entering men's public and social world, as feminism has done to date, these stories concentrate on the fantasy of literally getting under a man's skin and trying on the constraints, freedoms, pressures, and powers that we have only imagined from the outside. In addition to trying out the penis as a ticket to maleness, many of the stories explore what happens when the penis finds itself in a female world—a place where it gets to stay after coming, goes shopping for health and beauty products, talks dirty with its girlfriends over lunch, and goes home to a pint of ice cream and a wardrobe crisis. The resulting collection is not so much a woman's head on a male body as a huge girlie erection with great hair.

In the 1988 documentary film *Dick: Women's Views on the Penis*, a number of women give one-line answers to the question of what they'd do with a penis, coming up with curiously disembodied answers: "Where would I keep it?" or "I've always wished I could sort of lease one and have it around whenever I need it." This book, for the first time, gives women artists free rein to explore the sexual fantasy in print, and an opportunity to reverse the drag queen phenomenon and parodically enter the habitats of men. The male English writer Will Self tried out a version of this fantasy in his novel *Cock and Bull* (1992), but his results were remarkably predictable, with the heroine inching closer toward sadism as her penis emerges and becoming a full-fledged serial killer by the time her manhood is complete; and the hero transforming into a nauseatingly perfect earth mother under the influence of his sensitive, life-giving vagina. Instances of imagined female-to-male travel have appeared occasionally in the last two decades as well—for example, Lynda Benglis's two-page advertisement in a 1974 issue of *Artforum*, which shows her fabulously athletic female body naked but for sunglasses and a massive, thrusting dildo. Novelist Sarah Schulman's lesbian fantasy "The Penis Story," which appeared in *On Our Backs* in 1986, tells of an unrequited lover who hopes the mysterious and sudden appearance of her penis will help in persuading her girlfriend to sleep with her. A fifth-century B.C. Greek vase in the British Museum shows a naked woman marching off with a giant phallus under her arm, presumably on her way to a party. Then there are contemporary art world examples of women portraying the naked male body, most notably the sculptor Louise Bourgeois in New York; the Los Angeles–based Plaster Casters of the 1970s, who specialized in casting the penises of rock stars; and the painter Sylvia Sleigh. But while these women look at men, they do not seek to enter or invade the male body.

When I was collecting the pieces for this book, I occasionally asked men what they would do if they were a woman who suddenly had a penis for a day. Except for a gay waiter in a Greenwich Village café, who, with an arched eyebrow, replied, "Whose?" I nearly always received the same answer: "Well, that's obvious; there's only one thing to do, isn't there?" This was also the response of Camille Paglia, a woman who has confessed to her masculine mentality. She said that if she had a penis, "I would go find Catherine Deneuve in a hurry." According to this view, to fuck a (preferably large) number of beautiful women (or men) is the point of being male; and, except when having unwelcome bouts of castration anxiety or impotence, most men seem to take their penis for granted. If the penis is considered at all, that's usually because it's not performing adequately or not getting enough. As Californian sex therapist Barbara Keesling once quipped, it's as though men think of their penis as a stranger letting space in their underwear.

Dick for a Day invites the male "member" in from its cotton-clad waiting room so that it is no longer merely a visitor or tenant. The contributors then observe its effect on personality, social interaction, and relationship to one's self. The results are startlingly diverse, from Mary Mackey's functional appliance that can beat eggs ("The Fun Dick") to Poppy Z. Brite's object of pure love; there is polymorphous appropriation at one extreme and awe-inspired worship at the other. Resentment at the power of the penis to justify arrogance and bestow privilege is also present in some stories, from Gretel Killeen's "Superdick" to Janice Eidus's "Snow White and Her Seven Dicks"; while other writers, like Jennifer Blowdryer and Amruta Slee, choose to explore what kind of man they would be. For many contributors the fantasy is not fueled by anger so much as by curiosity: as Janyce Stefan-Cole's story asks, does possession of a penis turn the world into a Raymond Chandler movie, or the bedroom into a farcical minefield? Other writers, such as Ginu Kamani in "Swollen Tide" and Kerry Greenwood in "Salmancis," explore myths of physical transformation, while Ava Chin looks into Asian-American castration anxiety in the context of cultural displacement. Optimistically playful in a Manhattan setting is Catherine Texier's "An Evening at the Royalton," in which the heroine seizes the opportunity for high-camp indulgence, sinking into imagery of soft flesh, clothing, chocolate, and the luxuries of Midtown seduction.

Outside pornography, the penis is rarely rhapsodized about, philosophized upon, or made a subject of love. And even within pornography, it is as often a weapon for punishment or revenge as it is a slave, provider, or tool for pleasure. Although the penis has received some well-deserved bad press in its time, the absence of aesthetic appreciations of the penis can only be a cultural loss. Ancient Greek culture not only satirized penises in the form of the satyr (from which the term "satire" derives its modern meaning), it also honored the penis as a symbol of fertility and eros, and as an object of beauty in its own right. In our own post-Victorian age, the twin Christian inheritance of pride and shame encourages mystique; images of and references to erections are among our strongest remaining taboos. The mass media underscore the most obvious absence: the ubiquitous, explicit sex scenes focus on women instead. In art galleries, too, the female nude continues to monopolize the voyeuristic gaze. Even more taboo are representations, however subtle or indirect, of a man coming. Despite the overload of clichéd symbolism to portray phallic worship and ejaculation—athletes scaling mountains; exploding fighter planes—the body, face, and gestures of men at the moment of ecstasy are sadly missing. While a woman's orgasm is dwelt upon in Hollywood movies in loving detail, and her pleasure exaggerated in audio overdrive, a man simply gets it over with like a featureless, worked-out machine. His achievement is in giving himself, erect and abundant, to the woman of the moment, or claiming her as conquered territory; but beyond the assumption that this is a triumphant event for any man, no one cares to ask if it was good for him, too.

The lack of interest in the finer details of male sexual experience isn't due so much to neglect as to an assumption that men prefer doing the looking to being looked at—or don't like to own up to it if they do. While the mouth and legs of the woman are open, invariably her eyes are closed.

Dick for a Day reverses this pattern, as women get to watch—parading as themselves, as men, and as whatever may lie in between.

The only counterbalance to date for the penis taboo have been a small selection of anthropological tracts, a blowout in the budget for exploring deep space, and a certain amount of feminist raillery. Second-wave polemicists, such as Phyllis Chesler and Andrea Dworkin, describe the penis as a totem of destruction, either the literal weapon of rape or the primary symbol of male domination. Much of this writing has been feminism's most excessive, poetic, fanciful, and aggressive, as if all women's resentment might effectively be aimed at this one offensive weapon. Recent feminist theory regards the phallus more abstractly, as the origin of law itself, the symbol of logic, hierarchy, and patriarchal order. Revising Freud's inadequate theory of penis envy, the French feminist school argues that the penis symbolizes a passport not only to hallways of material power, but to the basics of our culture—most notably its language, philosophy, and literature. More voguish are the evolutionary psychologists, who propose that biological differences have hardwired sexual interests into opposing camps that refuse to budge, even though they originated in long-outdated caveman scenarios. In the age of cybersex and synthesized on-line identities, this last notion seems the most pessimistic of them all.

These theories share a weakness: the assumption that the ownership of a clitoris or a penis signifies—and will always, inevitably, signify—an opposition of experience and a conflict of interests. In *Dick for a Day*, Pat Califia's essay "Dildo Envy" argues that if we reject this formula as incomplete, and push for the acknowledgment of more than two gender-based options, the deadlock might resolve itself into more interesting and conciliatory combinations. This has been my hope for the collection as a whole: to promote a more authentic interaction between the sexes by imagining the multitude of experiences that can arise from masquerading in each other's worlds. In a period of AIDS-related caution that has spilled from hygiene issues into moral imperatives, and at a time of conservative backlash claiming that feminists are puritanical and antimen, *Dick for a Day* also affirms the humorous and adventurous dimension of sexual politics.

Virginia Woolf wrote that men need women to act as their mirrors, reflecting an image of themselves twice as large as they really are. In *Dick for a Day* women get to parade before the images that men have thrown back to them, and reflect on images of themselves as they are refracted via the male surface for their own amusement. In the hall of mirrors that results, neither sex gets to be merely the audience, and all our projected images and fantasies are nothing but interpretations.

DICK FOR A DAY

Snow White and Her Seven Dicks: A Fairy Tale of Tails

JANICE EIDUS

The walking, talking, detached dicks of seven Rock Stars, past and present, are lined up outside my hotel suite, which is huge and magnificent. My four-poster bed is king-sized. My windows reveal a view of the city at night, stunning, aglow. A chandelier on the ceiling glitters.

Room service is in and out, bringing me the best champagne, the most flavorsome caviar, the sweetest chocolates bursting with the juice of cherries.

The reason I'm here, in this luxurious hotel overlooking the park, is because I, Snow White, the Beautiful and Famous Bestselling Novelist, am touring the country on a multicity book tour, and today is a special day. Today is the day my most recent novel, *Hot Spot*, is Number One on the Bestseller List. Until today, I've been number three, and number two, but never Number One.

The reason the dicks of seven Rock Stars are lined up outside my hotel door today is simple: They're my reward for being Number One.

🎎

Years ago, long before I ever dreamed of becoming a Beautiful and Famous Bestselling Novelist, *I* was the one waiting in line outside the Rock Stars' hotel rooms, along with hundreds of other nubile, horny, desperate female groupies. While we waited in line all those long hours, we spoke only of our unrequited, passionate love for this or that Rock Star, of how we yearned, desperately, to be the sole object of the Rock Star's desire.

When we were lucky enough to be one of those chosen to enter the Rock Star's room, we obeyed commands: Lie still, Spread your legs, Blow me, Bite me, Ram me, Suck me, Eat me, Bend over; Do it with my manager, my roadie, my brother, my walleyed, illiterate childhood best friend. We performed for them in threesomes and foursomes, with men and women. We danced naked, we hung from the ceiling, we cleaned up their puke, we cooked up their heroin for them.

Or, well, the *others* obeyed these commands. I never got further than a few French kisses, a quick hand on my breast, a peek under my ruffled panties. I, Snow White, had gotten a reputation as the Virginal Groupie. It started when I was twelve, standing on my very first line outside a hotel door. I'd confided in the others that I was still cherry, and word got around to the Rock Stars and that was that. I became an object of curiosity. Not that there weren't lots of other prepubescents hanging out, sometimes jailbait even younger than I, and the Rock Stars didn't hesitate to give those girls all the dick they had. But those girls had all "done it" before. About me, they'd say, "Uh-oh, it's Snow White, the Virginal Groupie," and they'd bounce me on their laps, affectionately tweaking my nipples and patting my butt, before they called in the next girl standing outside the room, usually an eighteen-year-old, six-foot aspiring model from Wichita.

The Rock Stars always insisted I remain to watch. This excited them even more, having the Virginal Groupie as their audience. I sat quietly on the sidelines, desperately wishing that *I* could be the one tied to the bed, that *I* could be the one being hit over the head with a bottle, having hot wax poured all over me, spreading my legs for the Rock Stars' dicks.

⚘

All we groupies ever really wanted from the Rock Stars was four things, which didn't seem too much to ask. We wanted them to perceive us as individuals, not as nameless, faceless sets of tits and asses jumping at their commands. And we wanted them to reveal intimate, true things to us that they'd never before revealed to a living soul, the things they didn't dare tell *Interview* or *Rolling Stone*. We wanted expensive, gaudy presents. And, finally, we wanted those Rock Stars to fall madly in love with us, so that after our one night together, they'd be changed men, yearning, pining, and lusting for us. We wanted them to return to their homes in Malibu and St. Tropez and to write the greatest songs of their careers for us.

We wanted them to marry us, and never to sleep with anyone else as long as they lived.

But we never got those things. Whenever the Rock Stars
fell in love, it was with assorted socialites, actresses, or models with names like Tisa, Tara, and Tiara. It was never with
me, Snow White.

🜊

But that was then. This is now, and there are seven Rock
Stars' dicks lined up outside my hotel room door. I'm the
Virginal Groupie no longer. I'm the Beautiful and Famous
Bestselling Novelist with the Number One Book, and I gave
up on Rock Stars years ago. I grew tired of yearning for the
unattainable, for men who thought only with their dicks. *I*
wanted to be the one in control. *I* wanted power. So I rein-
vented myself. I got myself a literary agent and began writing steamy, sexy books. I've been around the block plenty of
times since then—and, believe me, I'm never the one left in
the lurch, yearning, pining, and lusting.

Still, in honor of my days as the Virginal Groupie, I've
tied my hair into two girlish pigtails with pink ribbons. Apart
from these two ribbons, though, I'm unadorned, stark naked,
ready to greet the seven Rock Stars' dicks in my birthday
suit, the way they so often used to greet me. Because I'm a
Beautiful and Famous Bestselling Novelist, I can afford to
work out with a personal trainer and to eat the best and
healthiest foods. My breasts and thighs are perfect. My body
is bathed in an earthy, musky scent. My eyes are bedroom,
come-hither eyes; my lips are lush and pink.

"Well," I say, loud enough for the seven dicks to hear me,

from my prone position on the king-sized four-poster bed, "which of you shall be first?"

I hear cries of "Me!" "Me!" "No, me!" outside my door. I wrap my tongue around a chocolate. I take a sip of bubbling champagne. Giddily, I call out, "Let's start with an Oldie-but-a-Goodie, one of the older dicks. No," I amend that, "*two* Oldies! Salvatore! Curtis Lee! Come in here!"

And in they come: the dick of Salvatore, the pompadoured Brooklyn-born rocker from the fifties, lead singer of Salvatore and the Six Stars, heartthrob of city girls everywhere, side by side with the dick of Curtis Lee Grant, the raw country boy from the Deep South. These are their youthful dicks, of course, from when they were at the heights of their singing careers, before Salvatore grew fat and Curtis Lee grew too skinny, bald, and alcoholic. Salvatore's dick walks just like a Brooklyn boy: tough and swaggering. Curtis Lee's dick swings raunchily from side to side, mimicking the way his whole body moved back when he opened for Elvis, playing those Southern honky-tonks, long before either of them got rich and famous and inspired teenage girls everywhere to swoon and sweat.

They climb up—six inches each, at least, maybe seven—onto the foot of my bed and stand erect, alert, gazing at me with awe, reverence, and lust.

"Yo, Snow White, I love your books," Salvatore's dick says gruffly to me in his thick Brooklyn accent. "They changed my life."

"Honey, your beautiful, sexy novels about the trials and tribulations of contemporary women and men make me bawl like a baby," drawls Curtis Lee's dick.

They both hold out copies of *Hot Spot* for me to sign. "Maybe later," I say coolly. I lie there, legs apart, naked, stroking myself, playing with the pink ribbons in my pigtails.

The next thing I know, Salvatore's dick has scampered up between my breasts and is rubbing me hard, and Curtis Lee's dick is down below, burrowing inside me, a little locomotive of lust. Salvatore's dick bites my nipple, gently, then harder. Curtis Lee's dick expertly plays with my G-spot. I'm enjoying myself, but I've also got other things on my mind, more important things. Like how to dress for my next TV interview, and how to spend all the royalties I'm earning. Just the way they used to have more important things on their minds back then, when, even as the other girls were obediently biting and sucking, and I was obediently watching, they were on the phone with their managers, setting up tour dates and arguing over the cover design of their next album.

"Okay, boys," I say, yawning, "that's enough. Sing for me."

Right on cue, Salvatore's dick, perched on my left breast, breaks into a heartfelt rendition of his biggest hit, "Coney Island Cutie." Curtis Lee's dick, standing up tall and proud at the foot of the large bed, huskily croons "Mint Julep Eyes."

"Not too bad, boys," I say, yawning again. "Now tell me a secret."

"I'm not really a poor boy from Brooklyn," Salvatore's dick admits, shamefaced, still perched on my breast. "I was a rich kid from Scarsdale."

"And I didn't grow up in the cotton fields," Curtis Lee's dick mumbles. "My dad's a Harvard grad."

Meanwhile, I hear shouts outside from the other dicks who want their turns. I send Curtis Lee's and Salvatore's dicks on their way without signing their books, or even saying thank you. I remember exactly how it's done.

⚙

"Okay," I say loudly, "Rick and Slick, next!" And in they march, the little dicks of Rick and Slick. These dicks, too, are youthful, from the seventies heyday of the cult-inspiring heavy-metal group Mother Load, before Rick's face got pudgy and bloated, before Slick began looking like an aging hooker with a bad wig. From my days as the Virginal Groupie, I vividly remember Rick's fondness for whips and chains, and how he liked to be the one in control, spanking the girls. To show who's boss this time, I tie the two dicks to the doorknob. I'm all-powerful here. I call the shots, Gulliver in the land of the Lilliputians.

A long, thin whip, coiled in the closet, is waiting for me. Without any hesitation, I give Rick's dick a light smack here, and Slick's dick a light smack there, and then I smack them both just a tad harder. Between grimaces of pain, they harmonize on "Hey, Girl, Get Goin', Fast," Mother Load's interminably long rival to Led Zeppelin's "Stairway to Heaven," while I keep smacking. When I can't bear to hear the chorus one more time, I untie them and put down the whip. "Pretty good, but watch those high notes. And now, a confession from each of you," I demand.

"Sometimes I can't get it up," says Rick's dick, sadly, rubbing his wounds.

"I can *never* get it up," says Slick's dick, looking at me

with great big puppy-dog eyes, and holding out a copy of
Hot Spot for me to sign, which I ignore, of course.

🧑

Next, I opt for Bobby London and Sig Rooster. In sashays
the skinny, pouty dick of the freckle-faced Bobby—whose
career, like the Beatles and the Rolling Stones, began in the
dark, smoke-filled clubs of Liverpool—and the manly,
chocolate-colored dick of Sig, the Afro-haired, flower-and-
bead-wearing San Franciscan guitarist whose signature was
the peace sign he made with his gorgeous, agile fingers at the
close of every concert, melting the hearts of sweet young
things everywhere.

I turn over onto my stomach. Together, Bobby and Sig
enter me from behind as I bark commands: "Faster!"
"Slower!" "Gentler!" "Rougher!" "There!" "Not there!"
"There!" We do this until I hear them panting with exhaus-
tion. "Boys," I murmur, "it's show time."

Bobby's dick goes first. He sits lightly on my butt and de-
livers a soulful rendition of "Lovely Ladies," the soft ballad
that stayed at number one for over a year.

Then Sig's dick whips out a guitar from somewhere. He
stands on my shoulder with military bearing, and using his
little teeth he plays a riveting "Star-Spangled Banner," to
express his fierce allegiance to me. His version may not be
quite as good as Jimi's, but it's still pretty damned good, indeed.

"What have you got to say for yourselves, boys?" I ask,
after Sig's dick takes a timid little bow.

Bobby says, pouting once more, "These thick, luscious lips aren't all mine. I use collagen."

Sig slumps his shoulders. "I was really a hawk, not a dove. All that peace and love stuff was bogus, just a way to get girls."

"Oh, well," I say with a yawn, ignoring their pleas for me to sign their copies of *Hot Spot*, "see ya sometime, boys." And off they go.

In struts the seventh and final dick of the day, all by himself, the black-haired, big-shouldered, beer-bellied Gavin Later, the self-proclaimed "White Trash Bad Boy of Rock 'N' Roll," known for his misogynistic tirades, drunken brawls, and no-show concerts. His startlingly teeny-tiny dick boasts a fetching tattoo of me—Snow White, the Beautiful and Famous Bestselling Novelist—right on its tip. I lie on my back, knees up. He enters me fiercely, then pulls out all the way, then comes back harder, just the way I like it. Since his dick is to be my last of the day, my final reward, I let myself go. My orgasm is the stuff that wet dreams are made of: I heave, I gasp, I writhe, I moan, driving him all the more wild. We come in unison, also the way I like it. Still, I yawn very loudly afterward, because that's the way the game is played. "Sing for me, boy," I say, through my yawn.

Obediently, he sits on my pillow, swinging his legs, shouting the words to "Bad, Badder, Baddest Bitch," the song that catapulted him to instant fame.

"Stop. It's Revelation Time," I command, interrupting him midsong.

He runs around my bed, jumping back and forth, a zigzaggy, manic path. "I identify more with the sensitive female characters in your novels than with the insensitive male characters," he says, landing on my pillow. "And I like to wear women's underwear," he adds, swinging from one of the bed's four posts. I don't sign his copy of *Hot Spot*, either.

⚘

When it's all over, I send the seven dicks away, despite their tears and protestations. I call for room service, and more bellhops arrive with more champagne, more caviar, more cherry-filled chocolates.

I modestly pull the covers up to my chin as I sip and eat, while another group of bellhops brings in the gifts the dicks have left for me outside my door: a diamond ring, a bracelet made of emeralds, the deed to a brand-new house in Bel Air. I'm unimpressed. As the Beautiful and Famous Bestselling Novelist with a Number One Book, I can buy these things for myself.

The notes attached to the gifts profess the Rock Stars' dicks' undying love for me. I toss both the gifts and the notes aside. I stand up, untying my pigtails and discarding the pink ribbons. I comb out my hair into sophisticated waves, and I put on my clothes, the kind of clothes a Beautiful and Famous Bestselling Novelist like me wears: a black silk slip of a dress, a tailored jacket, high-heeled shoes.

As I dress, I smile to myself, imagining the seven little dicks strumming their guitars, singing their songs, yearning, pining, and lusting for me, weeping, wailing, and shriveling up. I imagine them reattached to their owners, sitting at night with copies of my books in their laps, rereading my words, remembering, forever, our one night together. I imagine them growing depressed, canceling tours, spending the rest of their lives on the verge of suicide. I imagine them getting arrested and being hauled off to jail for trying to climb over my back fence, even though I've taken out a restraining order against each of them.

I've had those Rock Stars' dicks once. I don't need them again. They were groupies, not to be taken seriously, just today's reward for being Number One. I'm Snow White, the Beautiful and Famous Bestselling Novelist. I can have any dick I want. And besides, I'm going to be very, very busy, writing my next novel, the one destined to sell more than all my other books combined, the one I shall title *Snow White and Her Seven Dicks: A Fairy Tale of Revenge.*

First of all, I'd want to have a big one—and I'd show everybody.

I think there are two ways I could look at it. If I had a penis, sexually speaking, I would have the ultimate sexual experience with a woman. I would surrender myself and ask her to tell me whatever it is that she really wants me to do, and I'd do it. But if I had a penis just for the sake of it, I would like to see what it's like to be a man, to feel his adrenaline and get inside his head, just to see what a man feels and thinks throughout the course of a day. I would like to see if having a penis really makes all that much difference.

Penile Infraction

VICKI HENDRICKS

I opened my eyes. Bright sun splashed across my rib cage. "Enzo," I whispered.

He was on his stomach, head turned to the wall, thick black hair swathing the pillow.

I sat up slow, moved nearer, put my face over his ear. The eye I could see was closed, the curly eyebrow in disarray. I heard his heavy breath, smelled it—sour Chianti from the night before. Hangover city, with dry mouth and coated tongue, no doubt. Oh, well—I didn't plan to kiss him.

I got to my knees and stripped the sheet past that soft furry crease beneath his buttocks. I drew saliva and dribbled it out over my fingers, poked through the red pubic hair into my labia and felt for my beautiful mini-weenie, my magenta Crayola. I trembled with sensation as I ran it out with my fingers, a turgid three inches from base to tip, not impressive in size, but stunning adjacent to a vagina.

"Ramona Romano," I crooned to it—to her—as I stroked. "You're all you wanna be." She was more me than any other part. I'd raised her on the steroid Dianabol, trained her to perk up to attention with a fingertip flicker or a fantasy slipping behind my eyeballs.

I opened Enzo's cheeks and plugged him before he could think, my Crayola spiraling to relax the soft drawstring of his crepey rose anus.

He groaned. "Christsakes, Mona. I'm still asleep."

"Stay asleep," I said. "I don't need you to move."

He coughed, tried to roll onto his back, but I pinned him, used muscle. He needed firearms if he wanted out from under me.

I leaned into his lumbar and slapped his cheeks with my pelvis in a rhythm plus a slurp.

A hand went to his forehead. "No, Mona. Mona."

"I'm coming, coming," I said. "Coming, coming. You can't stop me." I slowed and relaxed. I felt the juice drooling down the inside of my thighs as if it came from the tip. "Was it good for you, babe?"

No answer. Oh, well, I didn't need him to talk.

I rolled off, but I wanted more. I sat back on my heels and pondered his beautiful curves.

He reached for the sheet, pulled it up on one side, tucked it between his cheeks. He was either concerned about chafe or hinting for me to leave him alone.

I started to walk my fingers from the back of his knee to the inside of his exposed thigh. He was more interesting than the Yellow Pages. I crept right up to his pruny testicles.

"Do you ever get enough, Ramona?"

"Does anybody ever?" I said. "It doesn't run out—the more you get, the more you want, the more you can have." I put my face between his legs, licked the path of my fingers.

"You're an animal," he said.

I thought about that. I pictured two dogs I had seen stuck together in the road, the one on top a barrel-chested, black-furred terrier; on the bottom a wispy-haired Irish setter. They had no choice of positions, whereas I had all the options.

Enzo's eyes were closed again.

"You don't need to watch," I said. I picked at the sheet carefully. Pulled it tuck by tuck from between his buttocks.

"Uh-uh," he said. His hand went back and swatted across his cheeks like he was shooing flies.

I got up, swung my leg over him, and sat down.

"Umph."

It was the sound my friend's collie made when he dropped to the floor. Why was I fixating on dogs? I had always been a cat person.

I ran my fingers over Enzo's downy rounded glutes. "Nice ass," I said.

He groaned, mumbled something into the pillow.

Whatever it was, I wasn't interested.

He raised his head. Opened his eyes to slits. "Less is more."

Was he crazy? It didn't matter. "Too much of a good thing is wonderful," I said. "Mae West."

"Why don't you go have breakfast? Let me sleep for once."

"I'm not in the mood for food. Since when don't I let you sleep?"

He opened his eyes wide and rolled them.

"But if you want to eat me, it's okay," I said.

He lifted his head and took the pillow from under it, laid his head on the mattress, and put the pillow on top.

His naked body, without a head, taunted me. I couldn't take it.

I grabbed the pillow and flung it to the floor, stretched his arms above his head, and held him. I got my knee and calf under his hip and pried him over. I looked at his face. His eyes were open. He had given up opposition.

I draped myself flat on top of him, hip against hip, ding against dong, and got my tongue inside his mouth. Yep—sour Chianti. It didn't bother me. The heat began to generate, my sweat to roll.

I lifted up, and looked down. I was hard and small, and he was bigger but soft beneath me. There we were, pointing at each other. My magenta Crayola and his unloaded bazooka, side by side, equal at last. I had no place to put mine and he had nothing hard enough to put.

The sex sweat was still running behind my knees, but I gave it up. I let him go. He turned on his side and scrunched into the fetal position. For Christ's sake, I didn't need him to do anything. I was a perfectly balanced universe of one.

I went into the kitchen and searched for my Raisin Bran in the cabinet. It was huddled there in the corner, smothered by his stacks of boxes and cellophane-wrapped packages of spaghetti, linguine, fettucine, and angel hair. I swept them aside. A couple hit the floor.

I grabbed my cereal and poured it into a bowl, got the milk and sloshed it on the flakes, and gulped the rest.

I put the empty milk carton back into the refrigerator.

A Lewd Awakening

SARAH BOXER

THE MORE I PONDER IT,
THE MORE THE END INTRUDES
ON MY DAY OF EXTREME EXTRUSION.

INTIMATIONS OF MULIEBRITY.

HEY, MY DICK'S GONE!

I BEGIN TO THINK ABOUT IMMORTALIZING MY MANHOOD.

DADDY!

DADDY!

MOMMY!

Sarah Boxer

STILL, I CAN'T FOCUS ON
ANYTHING BUT THE END.
AND THE END MAKES
THE WHOLE DAY SEEM
POINTLESS.

THE SIMPLE PLEASURES ARE RUINED...

... AND THE HIGHER PLEASURES ARE INCONCEIVABLE.

Size and Sensibility

CAROL WOLPER

The surprising thing about shopping for a dick is that it's not all that different from shopping for a pair of shoes—except, of course, in one critical area. Size. Small is better on your feet, big is better between your legs. Or so it would seem, to judge by the women I saw at the Pleasure Chest, Hollywood's emporium of sex toys. The first thing I noticed was that these women were attracted to the good-looking big (but not huge) strap-on dildos. Comfort and style were obviously taken into account. Which makes sense. If you're going to walk around your bedroom, or someone else's, wearing one of these things, you want to feel as comfortable as possible. And female vanity dictates you also look as good as possible.

The reason I'm even thinking about women, dicks, and shoes is because I was asked to. Well, not the shoe part. But once the subject of having a dick for a day was raised, all kinds of ideas, images, and shopping trips came to mind.

Now, I understand that the rules of this fantasy don't limit me to reality. I could explore having a real dick. What girl hasn't, at some point, thought about what it would be like to be a boy? I have. But I do mean boy, not man. I thought about it back when I was six years old and Alfonse Isadore offered to show me his equipment if I showed him mine. Already the budding extrovert, he dropped his pants before I could reply, leaving me to conclude that although I coveted his baseball glove, I definitely had no desire for his other assets.

By the time I hit my teens, I had amended my position. Though I still had no desire for Alfonse's equipment, having unlimited access to what a few of the other neighbor boys were sporting was definitely appealing. But the distinction should be noted: I wanted to play with them, not be them. And that's the way things stayed until I became a Hollywood screenwriter and learned that though the pen may be mightier than the sword, the pen is definitely not mightier than the dick. Dicks rule in Hollywood. And who hasn't, at some point, fantasized about being a ruler?

It was a latent fantasy until this assignment encouraged me to imagine myself as one of the boys . . . at least for a day. Problem is, right away I got hung up on a very key part of this fantasy. What kind of dick did I want? My first instinct (of course) was to say a big, big dick. If I was going to be a guy, I wanted to be a tower of testosterone. But being a female all these years, I've found through experience and countless hours of girl talk that really big dicks can sometimes limit the range of recreation. So already I was having a dilemma. Should I opt for what would please my male ego or for what might please some girl?

Thinking as a guy, I had to go with the ego.

With this key part of the fantasy in place, I started imagining the effects this tower of testosterone would have on the life of a Hollywood screenwriter. And right away, it hit me . . . what a difference a dick makes.

⚨

Instant results, I'm walking different, talking different, and eating different. No iced tea–and–salad lunch for me. I get to eat real food, a veal chop (by the way, do women ever order veal chops? I've never seen one do it) and a side of roasted potatoes. I get to sit anywhere I want, no subtle or not-so-subtle maneuvering necessary. Like us guys don't know what the deal is when a woman turns into an NFL running back in order to score the chair with the flattering backlighting. But, hey, let the sun shine on my face. So what if the lines are beginning to show. What do I care? I'm a guy, and a nonactor to boot.

So there I am at this business lunch sitting across the table from a studio VP (female) who actually says she's "so glad I was available to catch up." (Where do they learn how to talk like this?) The thing is, she may have a big title but she's a wreck. I can see that she's thinking "Okay, I'm smart, but am I pretty?" She's checking her lipstick out in the silverware every five minutes and flipping her hair around like she's in some infomercial. She takes two bites of her arugula salad and goes through three refills of her iced tea. By the time we leave, she's jacked up on caffeine and starving. I walk out of there feeling good. Well fed and pumped. She's even more insecure standing out in the bright daylight as we wait for the valet to bring up the cars. Her sunglasses don't hide shit. So, as she's about to get in her BMW, I give her a break. I kiss her on the cheek, tell her she looks great and I look forward to seeing her again. A big smile breaks across her face. Sometimes this stuff is so easy, it's criminal.

Feeling like a player, I drive over the hill to a pitch meeting in Burbank. I'm sitting there with two Warner executives. Guys who don't often take this kind of meeting. Guys who are only interested in the big stars or the latest (male) new "genius" to hit town. Only through hype do I fall into the latter category, but these guys are hypemasters themselves. They applaud hype as long as at the end of the day it brings them one less headache and one more million. Hey, I know the rules of the game. Some writers might be intimidated by these guys, but not me. I take my cues from the guy who nailed this game three decades ago—Jack Nicholson.

Legend has it that back in his early days, before things got easy after *Easy Rider*, he was doing an improv in an acting class. When he finished, the teacher said, "There's nothing there, Jack. It's not working." And Jack looked up at him, eyebrows raised, big smirk, and said: "Did you ever consider that maybe it is there and you just can't see it?"

That's my role model. That's the way it's done. If you don't get it, fuck you, blindman.

But the thing is, these executives are into it. And it's not even an action movie. It's a fucking character piece. A fucked-up character, but still. It's the kind of story Hal Ashby might direct if he were still alive. I'm not saying it's *Shampoo* or

Being There, but it's got a message about this fucked-up culture and its fucked-up politics. It's also a movie with a great blow job scene.

These guys love it. They're laughing and schmoozing me and not taking any calls. They only have a couple of problems. Character pieces can be too soft. Too talky. "Hey, do I look like I'd write a pussy movie?" I say. That's all they need to hear. I'm a guy. I speak their language. They're reassured. A woman would never be able to sell this idea to this duo. They'd worry that it'd turn into *How to Make an American Quilt* for the MTV generation. And not only does that not sell tickets, it doesn't make them hard. By the time I leave there, though, I'm feeling pretty hard. It's a done deal. Now it's all up to the lawyers to hack out the details.

On the way back over the hill, I call my agent from the car phone and tell him we've got to meet for a drink. Now. I'm on a take-charge roll but I don't want to be an asshole so I say, "How about Barney Greengrass in thirty minutes?" It's right across from his office, so at the most it's just a major inconvenience.

He's already there when I arrive, drinking an Evian. I go for the martini. Vodka. Straight up. Three olives.

"How'd the meeting go?" he asks.

"This is how it went," I say, relishing my testosterone high. "I've decided I've got to direct this script."

He sits there, staring into his glass of Evian. I'm waiting for him to say, "But you've never directed. You've never been on a set." "Hey," he could say, "you don't even know how to put film in an Instamatic," and he wouldn't be wrong. But fuck it, so what, I'm a guy. Guys pull this shit off all the time.

"Okay, look," I say. "I know Nora Ephron had to be nominated for two Oscars before they'd let her behind the camera. So what. I also know there's a list of guys with no credits who got to call the shots 'cause they had the balls to hold out for the whole package."

He thinks it over, pushes his glass away. "It's doable," he replies quietly, and then signals to the waiter for a martini. But he's not drinking to celebrate. Just the opposite. With a director credit in the mix, he knows the deal's just gone from a sure thing to a maybe. But so what. Fuck it. That's the way the game's played.

I walk out of there feeling pretty good. Having a dick is great, I'm thinking as I ride down the store elevator. I'm also thinking about the night ahead. What kind of girl do I want to hang with? Whoever she is, she's got to be a girl who knows how to worship the dick. Just then the doors open and there I am on the main floor of Barney's. Confidently, I work my way past the cosmetics and jewelry departments. And just as I'm approaching the back door, just as I hit the shoe department . . . the dick-for-a-day fantasy comes to an abrupt end.

⚶

It's over. All the estrogen came rushing back when I spotted the perfect pair of ankle-strap Manolo Blahniks. It was like I was Cinderella, except I found my own glass slipper. In fact, I found several. The Walter Steiger slingbacks. The short ankle boot from Robert Clergerie. Walking around in those made me feel like a real powerhouse. Nothing and nobody's going to fuck with my velocity in these. With the right boots and the right French lace G-string (lingerie, third floor) I'd be unstoppable. It'd be like having a dick without having to lug around the extra baggage. Which brought me to the moral of this fantasy. Cinderellas, take note: dicks are great, but never underestimate the power of the pussy.

1-800-YOR-DICK

SENATOR SIN

The sign said,
"Wanted,
volunteers
for scientific study;
we give
dicks
to women,
for a day.
Confidential results."

It was hanging
in the women's
bathroom
of a penthouse
restaurant.
I read it

while I stuck
a maxi-pad
in my underpants.

"1-800-YOR-DICK":
That's all
it said.
My date
was seated
at a window-
table for two
talking on
a cellular phone.

I sat down
and it rang.
He winked,
told his wife
he was working,
and hung up.
I picked up
and dialed
1-800-YOR-DICK.

"Yor Dick
at your service."
"You're giving out
dicks?"
"Small
medium

or large?"
"Medium, but
is that all?"

"Circumcised?"
"No, I mean
what do you
want from me?"
"You return it
in twenty-four
hours with
a full report."

"When
can I come?"
"You can come
right away.
Red
black
brown
yellow or
white?"

"I'm scared
of what I
might do with
a white dick."
My date asked,
"Who
are you

talking
to?"

"Your wife,"
I said.
His white cheeks
turned pink.
"I think
I'll take
a brown dick.
I loved one
once."

"Your dick
will be waiting."
I finished
my aperitif.
"There's pussy pie
for dinner
at your house,"
I said
to my date.

"What
is a woman
like you going
to do with
a black dick?"
He wanted

to know.
"Brown."
"Same difference."

"I don't know
but I'm going
to pick up
my dick."
I lied.
I knew
I was going
to fuck myself
first.

The box
was big
and heavy.
I carried him
on the subway
in my bag
and brought
him home
with me.

I locked
the door
and stripped
in front
of the mirror.

There
was me
and
my wet pussy.

I opened
the box
and picked up
my dick.
A bonus!
They gave me
a double dick
with balls!

My dicks
were beautiful.
I kissed
and caressed
and fondled
my dicks.
They danced
under
my fingertips.

I massaged
my face
with my dicks
and squeezed
each one
between

my tits,
and slid them
between my thighs.

I used them
to massage
my wet lips, rotating
my hips.
I sighed
and finally
spread my legs
wide.

I plunged
one dick
in one motion
to the hilt
and gasped
as I pulled
it out
and shot it
in again.

I looked
in the mirror
and saw
one hard
brown dick,
with balls
hanging down

between
my thighs.

I took him
in my hands
and started
pumping
as I knew
how to do.
This was new.
This was wild
and weird.

The phone rang.
I answered.
It was
my date's wife.
"I found
your number
in his pants.
I know
he's there."

"He's not here,"
I told her.
"But I have
something
even better
and I know
how

to use it.
Wanna come over?"

She took
a taxi.
I was waiting.
She was wearing
a miniskirt.
My dick
got hard.
I offered her
a drink.

I wondered
if her
pussy
was tighter
than mine.
My dick
got harder.
I put him
in her hands.

She admired
him.
He stood up
and pointed
her way.
She hiked up
her miniskirt

and jumped on
for a ride.

My dick
started dripping
sweet nectar
like
a breast
bursting
with milk.
I yanked him
out.

Semen squirted
all over
the mirror.
"That was
quick,"
said
my date's wife.
My dick
shrank.

Suddenly
I was sleepy.
She lit
a cigarette.
Someone knocked
at my door.
I answered.

It was
my date.

"What
are you doing
with my wife?"
"I fucked her
and now
I'm through
with her.
I have to
get up early."

I didn't see
his knee
but I felt
it hit
my balls.
He took her
and left
and I crawled
to my bed.

In my dreams
I punched him
and fucked
his wife
until she moaned
and begged
for mercy.

I came
on my sheets.

My dick
rose
with the sun.
I took
a cold shower
and decided
today
I would ask
for a promotion.

I bought
a new suit,
three pieces,
on my way
to work.
I went straight
to my boss.
I didn't waste
words.

"It's time
for you
to promote
me,"
I said.
"We already

discussed
this,"
he said.

"But now
I have
a dick,"
I said.
"What
are you
talking about?"
He laughed
at me.

"Let's go
pee together.
I'll prove it
to you."
When he saw
my dick
we peed together.
He promoted me
right there.

I felt good,
so I fucked
my secretary
on my desk
for an hour.

I visited
the men's room
frequently
to do business.

By the time
I returned
my dick
I had
passwords, perks,
and pertinent
information
I had never
even dreamed of.

I didn't need
my dick
anymore.
I kissed
him fondly
good-bye
and stuck
a fresh maxi
in my underpants.

Epilogue:

I got
the results
in the mail.

Apparently
most women
know exactly
what to do
with a dick
for a day.

A few
never returned
their dicks,
moved away
from family
and friends,
and are assumed
to be passing
as men.

GERMAINE GREER

What I would do with it if I had a dick for a day would largely depend on what kind of dick it was. If it was long enough I would probably try to find out whether I was as good/bad a fuck as I was reputed to be. If it came with all its attachments I would probably work on a sizable donation to a sperm bank, having failed to pass on my genes by any other method. The best bit would be getting rid of it at the end of the day.

Pick a Dick

LINDA GRAY SEXTON

Nineteen fifty-nine: I'm six years old, sitting cross-legged on the rough brown rug in front of the black-and-white television set in my parents' bedroom, entertaining myself with *Queen for a Day,* a game show, where powdered and permed housewives in flowered print dresses compete to be crowned. Each contestant pitches a lugubrious tale to the studio audience, detailing why she cannot survive one more day without the grand prize—which is always a large, shiny, new appliance that radiates power and heat from beneath its smooth skin of stainless steel. (Maybe Oprah got her start watching *Queen for a Day,* too.) At the end of each show an applause meter measures whose sob story is the audience's favorite, and the winner is bedecked with a rhinestone crown and a full-length velvet robe. Most important, she receives the prize she so desperately craves: a dishwasher, a washing machine, an electric stove with four burners and a deep-fry basket.

The contestants lick their lips, jump up and down, clap their hands, squeal with excitement; desire glows across chubby faces. No boredom here. Just pure lust. They don't seem much different from me and my friends playing Barbies. It's all fantasyland: everything you always wanted; everything you always wanted to be.

⚲

Nineteen seventy-eight: Nineteen years later. I'm lying on my back in a small tent in Acadia National Park, Maine. Sleep slides out of my reach as my boyfriend snores and several thunderstorms collide and crash above our heads. The quantity of rain that sluices down the hillside on which we are camped is astonishing.

My mother toilet-trained me by turning on the tap in the bathroom sink, and every time I hear the tinkling sound of running water I'm like one of Pavlov's dogs after the bell. Now I fervently regret the bottle of wine we had at dinner. I cross my legs, squeeze my thighs, curl my toes. I think of deserts, dry mouths, hot winds.

After a while, I nudge John. "I have to pee," I whisper.

"So go," he says sleepily.

"It's raining," I hiss, contemplating the logistics and wondering how wet the sleeping bag will be after I tromp out into the swamp of our campsite.

He's silent, listening. After a minute he says, "I have to go, too." And with that, he kneels in front of the tent flap, unzips the fly, lifts his penis in his hand, and pisses out into the night, a long majestic stream of relief.

I feel a flash of pure, unadulterated penis envy—envy of

such magnitude that Freud would surely applaud. My feminist bones despise John and his extremely useful dick.

Fifteen minutes later I uncross my legs and scramble for the opening.

"I'll dry you off when you come back," he calls helpfully as I stumble out into the dark to squat barefoot and bare-assed in the teeming mud. Water pours over my head, shoulders, breasts, back, belly, and thighs, and splashes up onto my bottom.

I return, shivering. John helps towel me down, but my side of the bag is soggy now, my feet are freezing, and I can't get warm. As his snoring threatens to drown out the sound of rain running against canvas, I ponder the unfairness of anatomy: anatomy is clearly not destiny, I decide, but it's definitely damned inconvenient.

I imagine what it would be like to have a penis, just for one day: No waiting in the serpentine line running from the ladies' room back to the entrance of the movie theater. No wrestling pantyhose over your hips while breathing through your mouth in the Portosan. No scrooching over a urine-splashed toilet seat and praying for balance. No pant cuffs wet from the puddle of pee left on the floor of the airplane lav by the guy(s) with bad aim. No frantic search of your pockets and purse when you realize, too late, that the toilet paper dispenser is empty. No crossed legs on long turnpike treks. Just the side of the road, a bush in the woods, a French pissoir, a quick trip to the urinal. Oh, for a shake instead of a wipe!

When I was a little girl I longed to be the queen with the rhinestone crown, screaming in ecstasy over her new washing machine. Now that I'm grown-up I'd pick a dick any day.

Rise and Shine

YAEL KANAREK

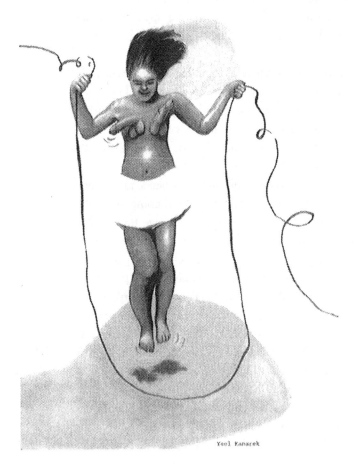

Yael Kanarek

There's No Such Thing as a Plaid Jockstrap

BELINDA LUSCOMBE

Eight A.M.: I woke up with a hard-on. This was not nearly as much fun as I thought it was going to be, although that was mostly my fault. I'd slept well, considering the monumental nature of what's happening to me. But I'd had weird dreams. Normally I dream about having sex with my boss or turning into an umbrella and protecting worms from falling hippos—you know, the same things as everyone else—but last night I dreamed about sport. Specifically, I was the end man in a closely fought tug-of-war. I was pulling and pulling, and when I finally looked up, the other team was the Chrysler Building. Worse still, just as I was making some headway I woke up. Immediately I regretted wearing my lace panties to bed. Justin likes lace panties, so it's kind of a habit. I can sort of see why he doesn't wear them himself now.

Anyway, after extricating myself, I poked Justin in the back, just as he has done to me every morning for the last seven months. Oddly enough, when the shoe was on the other foot, so to speak, he wasn't interested. In fact, he seemed vaguely repulsed. I guess that pretty well squashes the theory Marilu told me that her office manager told her about men who are obsessive about clean running shoes. On the other hand, perhaps I'm not his type. I was pretty disappointed—well, frankly, deflated. But it was just as well. I had only twenty-four hours with this little tyke and I had a lot to do.

Ten A.M.: First I wanted to write my name. This is something I've wanted to do ever since I was a child. I had four brothers, and every holiday they would have name-writing contests. If we went skiing they'd write in the snow, their urine making a little sizzling sound as they went. If we went to the beach they'd autograph the sand. My brothers have made their mark on the best resort communities in the fifty states. Try as I might, I couldn't get past two letters in mine, and even then I'd splash my ankles appallingly. I even tried writing it downward like the Japanese, but that's almost impossible to do in running script, and stopping between letters is not really an option.

Unfortunately, there was no snow or sand in our co-op, so I had to settle for the cat box. Oedipuss is quite persnickety, but I cleaned it out right afterward. Well, right after I took the Polaroid, anyway. Also, my bladder had been fuller than I imagined and I didn't pace myself too well, so my signature had more flourishes than usual. It still looked pretty good, except that when I tried to draw the umlaut over the "e," I splashed the carpet. Clearly, urine-writing isn't a precise art.

And Jodie was wrong. It's not at all like a tennis grip, fore-hand or backhand. More like snooker, if anything.

⚮

Eleven A.M.: Now I was ready to do what any red-blooded American girl would want to do with a new limb: acces-sorize. The cow at Bloomie's menswear hung up on me when I called to price lacy Y-fronts, so I decided to go for something a little more classical. I snuck a pair of Calvin Kleins—I think they're called grippers—into the dressing rooms at Charivari. They were so much more comfortable than my panties that I got overexcited and started jumping up and down and shaking it all about, which attracted the notice of the attendant. With a sour look, she told me it was store policy that transgender individuals buy any underwear before trying it on. I tried to explain that I was newly minted but she couldn't have cared less.

⚮

Noon: Next stop, the sports store. Who knew there were so many different types of protectors? Not many colors, though.

⚮

One P.M.: It seems Freud was right. I met a few of the gang for lunch. They pretended to be appalled when I told them of "the dramatic advance in my personal growth," but frankly, I detected envy. Eventually they got over it and started to get curious. Heidi kept asking me if she could try to arouse me—right in the middle of 69, where we have lunch so often the waiters can recognize whose cell phone is ringing!

Three-thirty P.M.: It was late by the time I'd answered everyone's questions and visited the Ladies' for show-and-tell
about seven times, and the Men's once, because I've heard
so much about the Men's at 69. Jodie stood guard, which
was just as well because even men with long-standing experience of penis possession have trouble finding the urinal
there. I'd never have found it if I hadn't accidentally leaned
against one wall while fixing my lipstick and activated the
electric eye that made it flush. I hope whatever they put in
that stuff washes out of silk. By this time I'd changed my
mind about the sex thing. It didn't seem fair that the one day
I could see what it was like for Justin, he begs off. I mean, if
he had what I (normally) had for a day, I'd try and oblige,
although unless it happened today, I'd have to be a lot more
imaginative than he ever is. But something was holding him
back. How could I help him get over it? Suddenly I had it.
He was afraid. I should have thought of it before, with all
those AIDS jokes Justin makes. "Girls," I announced to my
companions, "it's time to buy condoms."

Four P.M.: I wasn't sure, actually, that I wanted all my friends
along on such a sensitive mission. But when I saw the range
at Ye Olde Sheath Shoppe, I realized it was just as well.
These women are hardened purchasers and we had a lot of
material to sift through. There was one bad moment when
the store attendant asked us what size we were looking for
and I said small and they all said extra large, but we got past

that. It's so typical of our male-dominated commercial world there's such a range in condoms and nothing at all to choose between feminine hygiene products. There's every color, texture, thickness, shape, size, and flavor (not that you'd necessarily want flavor in a tampon—but, hey, it's nice to have the option). There are musical ones and ones with bits that hang off them. There are ones made of animal parts and ones made from chemicals. And all so charmingly packaged. I began to wonder if anyone wore condoms even if they weren't planning on having sex, just for the look of it. The salesclerk's expression, when I asked, seemed to indicate no. One curious thing: dozens of the packages talked about how Big Man condoms (and it's never Wee Willie or Pretty Prick or anything remotely whimsical) had the little pimples all over them for "her extra pleasure." If condoms were really designed with women in mind, how come we were the only females in the store?

✿

Seven P.M.: Stopped in briefly at the Cerise Cowboy bar to see if I was gay. Liza Minnelli was on the jukebox, which I liked; the lighting was low and romantic, which I also liked; and there were loads of cute guys there, which of course I liked. I was just about to go and talk to one when I realized there was a flaw in my logic. I decided to go home.

✿

Eight-thirty P.M.: Justin was already home, looking a little smug, when I arrived. I was nervously clutching a couple of shopping bags of condoms (better safe than sorry) and he was sitting hunched over in his big fisherman's sweater. Before I could say anything, he spoke. "I'm sorry about this morning," he said. "And to show you . . . to show you how much you mean to me, I bought you something." With that he yanked up his sweater and there they were, two of the perkiest breasts I'd seen since Gigi and I went skinny-dipping in the falls in Montana. I was a little nonplussed, actually, but kind of excited too. Also, I could feel something stirring underneath my skirt. "Gosh, um thanks," I started, but he cut me off. "Downstairs too," he whispered.

That was it. We were tearing at each other like roosters. Later—actually not that much later, to my chagrin—in the warm sleepy glow of the evening, he whispered, "I suppose I could get used to this."

"Why bother?" I asked, almost two-thirds overcome by a heavy need to sleep. "It's all over tomorrow anyway. That's why it's called Dick for a Day."

As I slipped into dreamland, I had the strange sensation that Justin was upset. What did he expect? I wondered. It was my first time.

I'd do exactly what I do now, and I'd live just as I do now. I suppose that's the best thing you can say, as I guess it means you don't need one, because it really has nothing much to do with adventure and strength.

Pact

LUISA VALENZUELA

I answered the telephone, and when I heard the long-distance beep a smell of sulfur hit me in the face like a warning. Even though the stranger's voice was not particularly cavernous, just metallic. But I recognized its guile, and I hadn't the slightest doubt that the devil was speaking to me, hidden for the occasion behind the innocuous oral disguise of a literary agent.

A literary agent, powerful, American. He offered to make a pact with me. I listened to him, feeling not curious but courageous: it is a well-known fact that the devil's cleverest trick is to make us believe he doesn't exist, so I proved he did by hearing him out.

The proposal had its amusing side: he offered me a noble, concrete dick for a day. In exchange for . . . ? I immediately asked him, being aware that these things never come free. In exchange for nothing, the Evil One answered me in his guise of a writer's agent with a honeyed tongue; it's matter of a literary experience.

A cunning trap, I thought to myself, because I know full well what a literary experience means, in every sense; I know to what extent the body and all the rest are involved.

The one on the other end of the line (where in the world, within or below the world, could he be calling me from?) overheard my thoughts, naturally, and hastened to reassure me:

"An experience lasting no more than twenty-four short hours—you write me the text recounting your sensations and that's it. It can be just one line or several pages, and afterward not the slightest trace of it will remain in your body. Yes, one: the pleasant memory."

"Does the organ being offered," I couldn't help asking, "come with all its plumbing, can it be employed for *all* its specific uses, will it fulfill all its functions, or is it only a decoration, a deluxe accessory, let us say, something that's only good for peeing standing up?"

"It comes complete with instructions for use if needed. Manuals, diagrams. It's not a copy, it's an original made to measure for you. . . ."

It must be granted that devils are practical. And they have a sense of humor all their own. Which explains why they're so attractive, so dangerous.

The idea was becoming more and more tempting, but I decided to take my time.

"Look, leave me your phone number, I'll give it some serious thought, and let you have my answer in a couple of days."

"Don't call me; I'll call you," the devilish devil said to me, and hung up without saying good-bye. It's unbelievable how closely devils resemble men.

The worst of it was that he left me unable to make up my mind about his offer and his call, because I kept mulling over all the possibilities and some of them nearly convinced me. From time to time, that is. In the sublime moments when I forgot all about prudence. When I told myself that in the last analysis, it was only a matter of dashing off a casual autobiographical piece and then fluttering on to something else.

After all, I had realized long ago that writing is always a pact with the devil. You have to renounce so many things and take risks when you are trying to do some serious writing. But not as much, never as much, and never as overtly as would be the case this time.

I recalled that phrase penned by a poet: "There are many slippery papers in the world that result in a fall straight to hell," and I didn't want to produce even one more of those toboggan slides of words. Well, yes, I wanted to want to, but this proposal brought me face to face with something different: slipping by way of one's very flesh, a change that was real, physical, hormonal, tangible, even aesthetic. What would I look like once I'd been turned into a man? Because having a cock wasn't enough by itself; it wasn't a question of being someone who'd had an operation, a part-time transsexual, to put it in the language of the devil who phoned.

But might this not be an old dream, and going through the experience be like having a dream rather than like realizing one? Yes, and after it had been written up what would I have left? I would still have the memory of it, and along with it, the beard and a bit of prostate or something of that sort that devils might forget all about and leave inside me, out of sheer carelessness, when they restored me to my original form.

All this without my even once pondering the question of where my own internal organs might end up during the metamorphosis.

Maybe everything will be replaced, so that there won't be any superimpositions and enough empty space will be available. These sex organs that configure me at present will remain in a sort of RAM, like the basic memory of an operating system on a computer. Plugging it into one of the organs of the opposite sex would be like activating the virtual memory that snoozes in every human being. It doesn't sound all that worrisome. Just a click, or maybe a double click, done from where devils have their domain, and then an undelete and that'll be that; he can forget all about me and just concentrate on publishing his anthology.

"All we want you to do is write us something for an anthology," the Evil One had explained from behind his mask as a literary agent.

They all keep saying the same thing. At this stage of the game I'm more or less fed up with commissions, requests, and projects. But this sounds different. More substantial, if it's possible to categorize it somehow.

That's the most frightening part.

The possibilities opened up by the project are endless. I reject some of them in horror; others delight me and I enjoy a great imaginary moment.

And then there's the temptation to have actual proof. Can it be true, can the phallic metaphor be felt as an object of one's own experience?

If only accepting the proposal sufficed to confirm the fact . . .

None of these considerations convinces me. That's why imagination exists: to put oneself in someone else's place without *being* someone else, with no need for disconcerting, demoniacal pacts.

Good sense wins out. As does laziness. Because it won't be enough to live the experience; afterward it has to be written up.

I wonder what made me think of the devil and not of God when I received the call. I know the answer: it would never occur to God to modify what He himself created in a certain definite form. Quite the contrary: God is somewhat narrow-minded about decisions He's made.

But I'm not undergoing an operation, I had told the caller who from now on we'll call the bidder. And he laughed as only devils can, leading me to understand that it was not a question of banal surgery.

Worse still. Even worse than virtual reality. It would be a realistic reality, the most threatening kind of all.

Yet it wouldn't be bad, right?: one of those nice fleshy dicks that can increase in size and weight. One that works well. A spirited one.

No way: the devil isn't one to give something away for nothing. It's anybody's guess what unspeakable fate will await my story afterward. What improper use it will be put to, what a pernicious influence it will have on the souls of young people.

A great deal more harmful—there are devils involved, don't forget—than any other piece of writing that has dripped from my pen. Who can tell, though; maybe the weight between my legs will make me sententious, moralistic. If in fact I have time left to write during the unprecedented twenty-four hours of being a man.

I doubt that I will; with a phallus ready for action I'll have more fundamental temptations, if the weight between my legs doesn't change my point of view and thereby instantly modify my language, the one being inseparable from the other, in which case writing would be a real challenge. But there will be so much to do in those twenty-four hours. Including going down to the street to pee against a tree, marking my territory. There's nothing to be lost by trying.

No. My scale of values is clearly defined. I don't need to go around trying to prove anything.

So when the phone rings I'm going to say NO, thanks very much but NO: I have my principles, I'm incorruptible.

And when the aforementioned telephone finally does ring, and the rather metallic, white-hot voice that smells of sulfur comes on the line, of the million questions I have, the first damned one I ask is:

"Are you certain the dick works at full capacity?"

"Quite certain. If not, what would be the point of the experience?" (The devil may have his defects but there's no denying he's logical.)

And without the slightest glimmer of the scruples that have been distressing me I say: "Yes, okay." And I accept because all of a sudden the thought occurs to me that five, ten, twenty years from now, at various times the phone will ring again and feminine voices, quite recognizably from this world, will remind me of a certain moment and a certain af-fair of the heart, a brief, intense moment shared with each one of them (some of them in the daytime, others at night) and they'll say to me: it bore fruit. Our love child is going to kindergarten, or to elementary school, or to college, as the case may be and depending on how much time has gone by. And I'll find myself with offspring I knew nothing of until then, progeny of mine at different stages of development, and even after I'm long past menopause, good-looking, grown-up, loving children, of my flesh and blood, will continue to turn up, as much my children as the two I have who were born of my womb, far more my children than my books.

And these new children of mine will not be able to accuse me of disaffection. Or indifference. I will just be their father.

Translated by Helen Lane

Salmancis

KERRY GREENWOOD

I thought of her as we lay, warm, in the darkness. Salmancis the nymph, pursuing the beautiful boy Hermaphroditus, inflamed by love, praying that she and her lover should be forever united. I knew how she felt.

Ah, the smooth skin, the deep chest, the fine bones of the man sprawled asleep in my arms. Not mine—never mine. I'm Dani the adventuress, I'm a night's amusement, a day's passing pleasure. I'm nothing permanent.

This one—ah, this one is different from the parade of the pretty boys. His name is Dion. Sleek as an otter, with green eyes like chips of emerald, strong fingers, a sweet mouth. His kisses are deep. I can feel his eyelashes flutter as he opens his eyes against my breast. My hand trails down the length of his body, curling into the scribble of rough hair at his loins, snagging on that which lies between us. He gasps, his mouth opening, sucks at a nipple like a child, more than half asleep. Heat floods me, surrounds us like a nimbus; we glow in the night.

Mighty gods of my ancestors, they say you were powerful: Hera, Hermes, Zeus. I make Salmancis' prayer. I cannot lose this one, this sleeping joy, this beautiful shepherd. I will sacrifice to you, recall your worship. Stir, Great Ones, from the darkness of Pluton's realm, from the necropolis, the city and kingdom under the earth. One calls who has descent and right; one calls who will believe. Give Dion to me forever.

⚘

Waking alone, as I had expected, I weep a little from pain, then rise, seeking tea. My hand slides down my body, cups a breast, scratches and yawns.

Stops yawning.

I throw aside the bedclothes and leap onto the cold floor to find a mirror. Long hair veils my face. I dare not pull it back. Because the caressing hand has found, under the swell of the breast and the cup-naveled female belly, a pole swollen with morning, a proud phallus.

Gods of the Night and the Morning, Achaean and Archaic, I have been heard. He is not here; he is inside me. I have his sex and he is inside my head. I can hear his voice, wailing, questioning, and I have no answers.

One hand grabs a breast, hard enough to leave red marks; his hand. One hand strokes a phallus, bringing a spurt of delight; my hand.

We lie down again to find out what we can do.

⚜

Dizzy and wet and rank with semen, we stand under the shower, listening to the voice of the water, desperately confused. We feel good together. My hand brings the phallus to climax, oh, strange feeling, as semen shoots out in a rush of fire. His hand caresses our body, pinching our nipples, stroking our thighs. He is exhausted; I am aroused. He has no more seed; I melt from the bones with desire.

We need to talk, but our voices are clashing, and in the back of our mind is someone else, some other singer, and we smell of crushed grapes and taste a faint tang of blood. We listen to the water falling as if it might resolve the voices before we lose our balance and fall, but they are louder and we stagger out and sit down on the floor, clutching our temples, weeping with our eyes, laughing with our mouth.

⚜

An hour later we are talking.

"I am Dion," he says, angrily, and I say, "I am Dani."

"We are us," he says. "I have gone mad, lying with you, Dani. If I ever regain my mind . . ."

"What will you do?" I ask, and I feel him laugh, my mouth curves.

"I don't know. All right. 'Why' will not get us anywhere, nor will 'how.' What about 'What are we going to do now?' "

"I don't know. This has never happened to me before."

"Ah." I can hear him thinking. His mind is fascinating. All straight lines. He catches my thought and comments,

"You think in curves, in loops—it's all convoluted. Lateral. Strange."

"You're just as strange to me."

"Did you really want me that much, Dani?"

"Oh, yes." I show him himself lying in my arms, and the glow of our heat.

"And I wanted you."

I can see a landscape in our mind. He is standing there, holding out his arms. I embrace him and we laugh again.

"Well, I've probably just gone insane, but while we're here, we might as well enjoy it."

"What do you want to do?"

"There is a number to phone. Ask for Hermione and Leander. They know me."

"Why should I do that?" I ask, nettled. I wanted his love forever, not an incubus giving me orders.

In response he shows me a picture so carnal that I catch my breath and make the call.

⚢

The young man Leander and the young woman Hermione do not know me, but he can convince them; he is a convincing man. They agree to lie with us. We have stripped our bed and we recline and watch them undress each other. They are beautiful, flawless; the young woman with cropped hair, so that the tender nape is visible. The young man with tousled blond hair, sun-streaked, which falls across his muscular shoulders.

They sit down to strip us, and we watch their faces as he finds the long straight legs of a man, hard to the touch, and she finds soft breasts and rounded belly. They lean and kiss, mouthing muscle and nipple, and our hands find a wet crevice and a bundle of soft genitalia which grows under our touch.

Someone has done this before. Hermione allows our mouth to find a pearl buried in folds; we hear her gasp, which he has heard before. Leander strokes our phallus, stoops to suck, and we feel our own flesh grow, blood pumping into receptive channels, which we have felt before but feels wonderful, oh, the flex of the pelvis into the caressing hand and mouth.

Then we lie over the woman's body, feel her thighs close on our hips, the hard muscle yearning toward her, feeling for a home. Ah, to plunge and feel her vagina velvet-soft, wet, a sucking, pulling motion, a movement like a rider's urging a horse over the line. We are arrived at orgasm, and we cry aloud.

I am unsatisfied; I watch the woman receive another lover, know the long heat which is building in her, the slow increment of passion, and hear her cry as the climax blooms around the penis.

I am fallen, spent, exhausted.

❦

We farewell the friends, shower again. Our clothes are not designed to accommodate a penis. We urinate standing up and splash the wall. He says, "Well, that was interesting. Now, how do I get my body back?"

"I don't think you do."

"But I can't live like this, stuck in the wrong body!"

"We will have to learn some way of living together," I point out, reasonably. There is the strangest flash of rage, which makes my fist form and beat at my breast; I make the hand fall. "We can't afford to hurt this body," I add. "It's the only one we have."

"I can hear what you're thinking." He seizes control of the mouth and I speak aloud, to the astonishment of the cat. "You did this on purpose. You wanted me to yourself. You prayed to the Greek gods to let you be always with me. And now look what's happened!"

"We suffer the fate of Salmancis," I agree, "because I loved you, and you were leaving me."

"I loved you," he says sullenly. "But I had to leave. You knew that. You said, 'I am an adventure.'"

"I spoke the truth," I say, and he laughs. There is something I want to know.

"Does it always feel like that, making love, for a man? Do you always just lose desire, once the seed has spurted?"

"Yes. Does it always feel like that for you, that slow buildup, that plateau where you can climax again and again?"

"Yes," I say, watching our hands assemble a meal. Our tastes are different. I wonder what our mouth is going to find acceptable. I bite into a black olive, then spit it out on an impulse of revulsion.

"Tiresias was right," he says. "I hate olives; isn't there anything else to eat?"

"Tiresias?" I ask, spreading cottage cheese onto a piece of rye bread and biting again. This goes down without complaint.

"He was half-man, half-woman, like us. He was asked who got the most from love, and he said women. I'm tired. I must sleep."

"I'm not." I continue eating. "I'm hungry."

The fist clumps again. I unfold the fingers. I eat the rest of the bread, and then he makes me sleep.

🜨

Five days later I am at the market. I am stronger than I was. My legs walk farther, my back can bear a greater weight. My pack is full of breakfast cereal and rye bread and cottage cheese, the only things we can eat. My phallus is misbehaving. Every time a pretty girl walks past, it stirs and presses almost painfully against its constraints. If I even think of sex it rises and nods at me. But I do not desire women; he desires them. When a beautiful young man smiles at me, the thud of lust that used to ground at the base of my spine diverts, and then is blocked; he does not desire men. I cannot sleep for thinking of him as he was, so male and beautiful. In my sleep I remember the delight I felt as I accepted him into my body, but I cannot reach my own climax, only the male one, which leaves me unsatisfied in a mess of semen. He is nocturnal; I like to get up early; we have only had four hours' sleep a night since the curse of Salmancis fell upon us.

In that sleep, I feel him weeping for his lost autonomy, and I join my tears to his as they course down our face.

🜨

I carry the cage home and stand in my own garden. I have constructed the altar as the classics textbook instructs. It is an *énagismos*, a hearth for the dead, and to the dead gods I must sacrifice. His hand holds a knife. I transfer it to my own. The funneled bricks will bear the blood down into the realms of the dead.

They coo as I draw them forth: two white pigeons. I cut my wrist and his, and drops of blood gleam darkly on the bricks. Then I pray as the book says, to the dead gods who stirred in their sleep to grant my prayer with such careless cruelty.

"To all the gods, to Hera and Artemis and Zeus all-father, to Heracles the hero and Hermes the messenger, this is the offering of Dion and Danaë, who regrets her prayer. Return us, Lords of Power, to what we were."

ㇼ

The neighbors found us before we bled to death. White feathers were stuck to us with dried blood. But we were lying—they said—as close as lovers, breast to breast. Dying mouth had kissed dying mouth, supremely, triumphantly other. I saw no chance, in that moment, of our ever being parted again.

The Lorena Poems

LYN LIFSHIN

Her Penis for a Day

it lay in my hand,
seemed to promise
there would be
sweetness if I

obeyed. I opened
the window, opened
my palm and thought
it would lift up,

like a dove, free. I
thought I could
fling it into the
night and it would

float up, become a
star, a light I'd
no longer feel the
darkness in, sure

as my name is
Lorena

Lorena Remembers the Night
She Had a Penis of Her Own

as unlike what it
was when attached
as a woman whose
life line to a ship
or a man is cut
and she flounders,
bloats, belly up
on the waves
of whatever holds
her, no longer
in control. It
flopped, a stranded,
desperate fish,
scared as I felt
when he came back
bellowing and wild.
The blob of lost
slippery skin

could have been me,
huddling close
to the edge of the
bed, afraid
not to give in.
I could have been
what I held in
my hand that night,
cowering, quivering,
coming apart tho
somehow, even
wounded, abandoned,
I made it too

Years Later Lorena Thinks of the Penis She Had for a Day

how, in her hand,
it was so much
less angry,
more like a
scared bird
not the weapon
she'd known
but shriveling,
scared, a wounded
kitten coiled
into itself, into
her hand as if

she were skin, a
caul it could
find refuge in,
not a fist
of blood, punching,
a sword of bone
and because it
seemed to
quiver, dream of
flight she'd
just let it go

KAZ COOKE

The Gift

———

KIM ADDONIZIO

I find a dildo on the street: thick and slightly curved, flesh-colored, dark fluff around the balls. It looks so convincing that for a second I think it's a real penis, and I feel a sense of vertigo. It's brand-new, wrapped in white tissue which has ripped open. There's a thin blue-and-white-striped ribbon tied around it, and red Scotch tape with little Christmas tree designs holding the corners. I look around to see if there is someone nearby who might have dropped it. The street is full of people entering and leaving stores, carrying oddly shaped packages or dragging enormous bags full of gifts, no doubt intended for loved ones—yes, it is clear that everyone but me has loved ones to buy for. The dildo could belong to anyone. It looks elegant and expensive and forlorn, lying there so vulnerably, perhaps about to be stepped on, trampled underfoot, a smudged heel mark left on the once-pristine tissue; perhaps it will be kicked aside, to lie all night beside a garbage can, or even placed inside with the reek of old hamburger wrappers to which well-chewed gray gum clings. I can't bear these thoughts. I bend down to cradle the object in my hand. I think for a minute of its rightful owner— perhaps some woman like me, a woman who is lonely, iso- lated in fact, a woman who has no one to be with at Christmas. Maybe she bought herself a present, a present she would wait until Christmas morning to open; maybe she would take it to bed and close her eyes and moan and rock back and forth on it, saying, "John, John" (for that is his name, the man who walked out on me at the start of the hol- iday shopping season, leaving me devastated, perhaps even suicidal; who knows what I may do next), and then she would come, her legs stiffening, her juices flowing, and she would begin to cry afterward and perhaps fling it across the room with a curse; but now I have deprived her of all that, I have picked it up and put it into the pocket of my long black coat and hurried home with it.

Now it sits—or stands, rather—on the dresser, freed of its wrappings. It glows in the light of the lamp; its veins seem to pulse; a rosy aura suffuses it. I take off my clothes and ap- proach it; something seems to radiate from it—a sense of ease and power, a kind of self-satisfaction, a kind of . . . lust—yes, it is clearly lust I feel. I seize the dildo in my hand, I fall to the floor with it and writhe around, it throbs under my palm, swells and hardens as I pump it faster and faster. My orgasm builds until I explode all over the rug; come spurts from me, one spurt, another, I lie exhausted holding it in my hand, I pass out from the sheer pleasure of it.

I wake up, not knowing how long I have been unconscious. Maybe minutes, but maybe years; I could be an old woman, finished with sex forever, content to sit on a sagging plaid couch and stare at the television in an ugly room with no visitors day after day; I eat candy bars from the vending machine, at night I take pills and lie awake listening to the radiator and the nurses' shoes going by my door and the person in the next room trying to breathe with his weak collapsed lungs. I stagger to my feet, feeling strange and dizzy, I look in the full-length mirror and see that I am not an old woman at all; I am a young man.

I have a large penis, thick and slightly curved, with dark hair around my balls. I yank at it and feel it at the base of my belly, I look at myself in horror. I would gladly turn into something else—a werewolf, a vampire, I would happily be like Gregor Samsa and live out the rest of my life as a dung beetle. But I am a man. And already, as I look at myself, the horror begins to fade; I can no longer think or feel anything but—yes, again it is lust I feel, I touch the head of my penis and it quivers, it longs to dive into the bedsheets and thrust, over and over, it takes me with it, I come all over the sheets, yelling and thrashing about.

Afterward I sleep deeply. I wake the next morning and think it has been a dream, perhaps I am delusional, perhaps the doctor was right after all and I should begin taking Prozac; but, truthfully, I feel better than I have in weeks, and besides, I have a hard-on; I lie there dreamily pulling on my penis, and come again in the sheets, which are already a little stiff and sticky. I think of doing the laundry—it has been so long since I have washed the sheets, or my clothes, or cleaned the apartment; I have been so depressed over John's leaving. But I do not want to clean today. No, I want to take a shower and eat a large breakfast and take my penis out into the world.

Now the streets look different, the shoppers so hurried, so pathetic in their desperate efforts to find just the right gift. I walk confidently, feeling my penis bulge against the zipper of my jeans; it is my companion, I will never feel lonely again, it will accompany me everywhere. I thank God for this gift of a penis, my beautiful wonderful penis, tucked so cozily inside my silk underwear, nestled like a little wren; I see an attractive man and the wren begins to grow talons, it lifts its great wings and follows the man with its fierce eagle eyes, it wants to swoop down and carry him off to my apartment and feast on him for hours.

I follow the man down the street, into a store where he fingers scarves, looks at expensive earrings, takes down pretty kimonos from a rack. I remember that I am a man, too, and suddenly a wave of revulsion rises in me, the thought of dragging him home with me is crushed and drowned by the wave crashing over it. I am normal, I say to myself, normal; there is nothing wrong with me, I have never been a woman or wanted to make love to a man, I must wipe all that from my mind—especially the image of sucking on a penis, the joy of taking it into my mouth, licking the clear liquid that forms a bright drop at the tip, swallowing the slightly bitter fluid as I kneel before John, as he strokes my hair and says, "Baby, oh baby"—I must erase all that.

I hurry from the store, and now I see the women, their breasts bulging inside sweaters or hidden under coats, their asses moving just ahead of me like beacons to guide me; I think of their cunts and their smells, their soft inviting mouths. The eagle circles and circles, hunger gnaws at its belly, and now a kind of terror: I must find a woman, a woman who will have me, suddenly my penis is profoundly lonely and cold and sad.

I go into a bar and the terror is greater; there are women here, all around me in twos and threes, my penis is about to leap from my pants. I want to go up to one of them, to lean her back over a table and plunge into her, but I must stop myself; I drink beer after beer to quell my anxiety, to try and think of a way to do this politely. I stumble to the back of the bar, into the men's room, stand at the urinal and watch the arc of piss, golden and fragrant, and I am so fascinated by it I forget about the women. I go into a stall and jerk off, sitting on the toilet, and then emerge calm and in control once more. I return to the bar and continue to drink. I talk to no one, I think bitterly about my life, my past lovers, I resolve never to love anyone again; somewhere in the deepest recesses of my brain I remember who I am. I know that something is wrong, but it no longer matters. I get gloriously drunk, so drunk that everything goes black and disappears. . . .

I wake up in a strange, prettily decorated, room. I am lying in a canopy bed. Tiny lights are strung around it, blinking on and off; Bing Crosby is singing "White Christmas," and I can smell sugar cookies baking somewhere. I want to reach between my legs to see if I still have my penis, but I can't move my arm very far. Perhaps I have had a stroke, and there is no hope I will regain my bodily functions; I am in a hospice, no one will visit me but volunteers doing their Zen practice, who will sit beside me to experience dying close up and tell me I must learn to let go. "Forget John," they will say; "Life is but a dream," they are saying, or someone is singing; yes, a little girl is singing "Row, Row, Row Your Boat," in a high, pleasant voice. Now she is standing over my bed, but her face is huge, impossibly huge; surely I am dying, and this is the angel of death, wearing enormous wings and a white gown and holding a plain wooden wand in one hand, a glittery silver star stuck to one end of it. She reaches down for me, and lifts me, naked, into the air. She sets me on the dresser, and I see in the mirror that I am supposed to be female, I have long slim legs, a tiny waist, but I have no nipples on my otherwise perfect breasts and nothing between my legs but a sort of hinge, no sex at all anymore. I try to open my rosebud mouth to scream, but it is painted shut, it smiles happily back at me. "Merrily, merrily, merrily," the little girl sings, and begins to brush my hair.

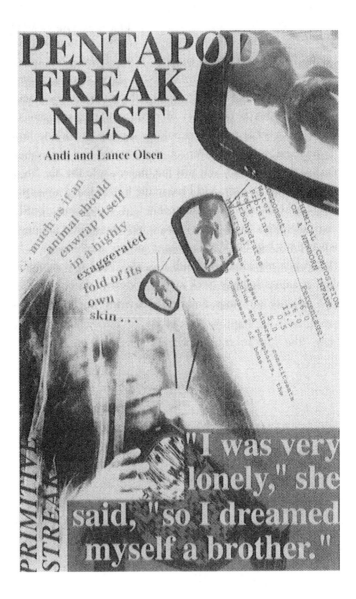

PENTAPOD
FREAK
NEST

Andi and Lance Olsen

... much as if an animal should enwrap itself in a highly exaggerated fold of its own skin ...

PRIMITIVE STREAK

"I was very lonely," she said, "so I dreamed myself a brother."

I remember the old Branden-
burgh Museum in Philadel-
phia where for the price of
one dime—ten cents—you
could see Jo Jo, the Dog-
faced Boy; Plutano and Wai-
no, the Original Wild Men
of Borneo; Laloo from India
with his twin growing out
of his body; Arthur Loose,
the Rubber-Skinned Man who
pulled out his cheeks eight
inches and let them snap
back into place; and the
famous Mrs. Tom Thumb. The
popularity of the freaks
carried the show but num-
ous vaudeville performers
not yet good enough for the
Palace or Roxy's in New
York, were used as fillers.
Among the people who got
their start there were Al
Jolson, Harry Houdini,
Buster Keaton and Van
Alsyne. . . . Though these
men did well later on, it
was always the freaks the
people came to see.
                —Daniel P. Mannix, Freaks:
           We Who Are Not As Others

**"Heart of my heart," she
said. "Mind of my mind."**

"The best part of the
dream was our new
Pentium processor."

the strange sex lives of Siamese twins

"The *body of the penis* is the part between the root and the extremity. In the flaccid condition of the organ it is cylindrical, but when erect has a ...gular prismatic form with rounded ... the broadest side being turned ...nd called the *dorsum*. The ...vered by integument, and ...ts interior a large portion ...bra. The integument ...enis is remarkable for ...ts dark color, its ...nection with deeper ...and its containing ...*Gray's Anatomy*

the human torso who could sew, crochet, and type

the dwarf clown's wife whose feet grew directly from her body

the tragedy of Betty Lou Williams and her parasitic twin

"We had always wanted to be freaks of nature, and now we'd got our wish."

affairs of midgets

LISA PALAC

If I had a dick for a day, I would no doubt wake up with a huge boner. I'd have to beat off. Despite my attempt to be quiet, the noise would wake up my boyfriend, who would ask, all coy and snuggly, "What are you doing?" A rhetorical question. He, being the greatest boyfriend in the world, would blow me. My first morning blow job. Now I would understand. I would also be amazed that I could come in about five minutes or less. Taking too long would not be my problem today.

Swallowing, of course, would be his.

Dildo Envy and Other Phallic Adventures

PAT CALIFIA

If I woke up one morning to find myself transformed into a
penis person, my first response would be a mixture of disappointment and anger. The transformation would feel like a
violation. I enjoy being a woman, albeit a woman who does
a lot of things that many people think are male. Virtually
every aspect of my life is organized by my gender identity
and by the fact that I am a woman who loves other women—
a dyke who does not give men much attention or space in my
life. I like constructing a *fantasy* of maleness for my sexual
partners. That way you can use all the fun bits and leave the
icky bits out. It's fun for me to figure out exactly what sort of
master, daddy, evil cop, decadent schoolmaster, or harem
trainer the bottoms in my life fantasize about. I can tell I am
getting serious about someone when I go out in quest of the
perfect dildo to fit her cunt. I've pondered various latex and
silicone appendages for upwards of twenty minutes, trying to

recall the specific characteristics of the new vagina in my life. Is she a girl who is narrow and deep, or one who is shallow and broad? Would that implement with the extra-big head give her goose bumps, or would she like the one with the slight upward curve? If I'm shopping for another dildo that will slide into her ass without a hitch—well, I'm about to get married. I am the vacuum cleaner of love, baby, brandishing an attachment for every sensual whim, like a sex-changing, thousand-armed Hindu goddess of lesbian delight.

Much has been made of the phenomenon of penis envy, which is supposedly the birthright of every woman. While I don't want to argue with Freud (it is notoriously difficult to win arguments with dead, famous white men), I do want to suggest that even if penis envy does exist, there is another equally potent, but much less visible complex, that of dildo envy.

There isn't a man alive who doesn't worry about his cock. Most of them have a simple form of this anxiety: they are secretly convinced it isn't big enough. Boys who are gifted with eight inches or more worry that one day, it won't get hard. Or it will shoot too soon. Or it will come down with some itching, burning disease that makes pissing a torture. Even men with big cocks that function as dependably as hydraulic lifts are still tormented by the fact that sometimes a dick gets hard for the wrong reasons, for the wrong person, or in the wrong situation. It's like a dog that can't be taught to heel.

Dildos suffer from none of these deficiencies. If one of my rubber dicks isn't long enough or lacks adequate circumference, it's easy to throw it over my shoulder, head for the stacking bins of sex toys, and procure another. Dildos don't falter or become feeble. Condoms don't faze them; they stay up as long as the girl around them is in a mood to keep on coming. The muss and fuss of ejaculation simply isn't a problem, although if squirting warm fluid is really a turn-on, there are models available that can suck up and expel warm yogurt like a water pistol. As long as you put condoms on your probes and then run them through the dishwasher between tricks, STDs are not an issue. And if my sweetheart fancies a double fuck, I don't need to take out a personal ad or prowl seedy bars to procure an extra cock for her, which will come attached to a warm body with its own emotional and social agenda. I can combine ass plugs with ben-wa balls with vibrating rotating poseable plastic phalluses from Hong Kong. We can start out small and gradually move toward the gargantuan, or vice versa. Is this America, or what?

While a lot of straight male hostility toward dykes is based on a fear of our fluttering tongues and clever lips, a lot more of it is directed at the fact that we find it so easy to provide penetration that is totally centered around the pleasure of our female lovers. The pleasure I get out of fucking a girl is largely vicarious. I do it because I like seeing and watching women come. There's no reason for me to do something to her that she doesn't like. My own sexual response cycle is not tied into using or taking; it's about discovery and giving.

You may think that only another dyke would find this an interesting and arousing way to spend an afternoon. But how many women would jump at the chance to have as many orgasms as they wanted with somebody who would give them exactly the kind of penetration they liked, exactly the way they liked it, especially if the person running the fuck knew where the clitoris is and what to do with it? Imagine being able to get fucked royally without any fear of pregnancy or disease or rape. I am willing to wager that nine out of ten heterosexual women would prefer cocks that behaved more like dildos, if it weren't for all the shit you catch for going gay.

Straight men secretly sense this possibility, the loss of feminine companionship because their equipment can't compete with that of any butch dyke with a credit card who knows the way to Good Vibrations. It makes them cranky. It makes them insecure. It makes them nasty to lesbians. So they churn out all this bullshit about how two women can't satisfy each other and how lesbian sex is infantile or ridiculous. In case that won't be enough of a deterrent, they also threaten visible lesbians with enough street violence and discrimination to make it very obvious that it's expensive and dangerous to cross the border into Lesbos. The fact is that if lesbian sex really were inferior or unsatisfying, women wouldn't bother. Female homosexuality would go away all by itself. The suppression of erotic dyke splendor is necessary because it is just the opposite of silly or second-rate: It's fabulous. Fireworks everywhere.

I'm telling you, it's dildo envy. Plain and simple. When the poor dears lean out of car windows and yell insults at me, it almost makes me feel sorry for them. As long as I've got a lead pipe up my sleeve, that is.

That said, let's imagine that I manage to work through my resentment and pique and don't simply spend my miraculous day of endowment in bed with the covers pulled up over my head. After taking a piss, my first order of business would be to make friends with my new body. Jacking off seems the obvious strategy for accomplishing that. I'd want to oil up my fist and wrap it around that brand-new piece of meat and find out what it feels like to have sexual sensations happening outside of and away from my own body.

The way we deal with the world is based on the metaphors we use to try to understand how consciousness inhabits the body. When I want to learn something new, I imagine myself as bringing that novel thing, person, or information closer to myself, and incorporating it into my being. I would guess that men (or, to be more specific, men who do not enjoy anal penetration) would see that process as going on an expedition to invade or penetrate and thus occupy whatever it is that they need. The problem is, if that is the way you get close to the things you need to know or the people you love, the minute the penetration is over, you lose contact. You become lonely. The penalty for male orgasm is to be cast out. The classic cum shot in porn films is an attempt to escape that sense of loss. By visibly leaving cum behind, the bearer of the phallus attempts to maintain connection and possession. But what I have learned or loved as a woman is always a part of me. It is, on a symbolic level, inside me. To be male is to be a perpetual stranger, always seeking out contact that cannot be prolonged indefinitely without a great deal of frustration. To be female is to assimilate, absorb, ingest, and incorporate. Men try to rule the world, while women simply become it. There is something tragic and also heroic about this male dilemma.

Though I don't think I would be having such grandiose philosophical thoughts as I was merrily jacking off in my warm, quiet bed. What would holding a cock do to the images that I create to turn myself on? My private dirty movies of let's-pretend are all heterosexual, simply because male-female sex seems so exotic and strange to me, a forbidden and taboo terrain. It's already unclear to me whether I am aroused more by the resistance and shame of the ravished maidens in my fantasies, or by the lechery and persistence of their seducers. If I were wielding the implement by which young girls are ruined and maidenheads are breached, wouldn't I be more clearly drawn to envision myself as the battering ram, the rake, the cruel boss who takes what he wants and never apologizes?

Perhaps. But sex seems to proceed paradoxically. I think it's entirely possible that my queer sensibilities would revolt at having the balance in my mental kingdom of smut toppled in favor of topness. It's much more likely that my psychic adult cable station would flip the channel, and I'd find myself watching mental movies about muscular young men being cornered and cornholed by the imperious coaches, domineering employers, incestuous fathers, and sadistic priests who had guessed their secret natures and insisted upon showing them where their erotic destinies were to be found—i.e., on all fours, with their heads down and their asses in the air.

Because you can bet that if I have to be a man, even for one day, I am not about to become a heterosexual one. How could I stand it? I don't know how *they* stand it. I realize I am making broad generalizations, and that there's this thing called the women's movement that has made some big changes in cross-sexual relationships. But my gut reaction is that straight girls are a pain in the ass. Yes, I've been stupid and done my share of courting and winning a few of them, just to show that I could. But I've never understood butches for whom a straight woman is the ultimate trophy, a fetish of such sexual power that they would march over a dozen good-hearted and good-looking lesbian femmes just to steal a kiss from a straight girl whose boyfriend would shoot them dead if he ever found out.

Men are not my favorite critters. Straight men can be crude, violent, hateful, misogynist, and insensitive. But they *do* things. They go out in the world and work. They make things. They compete with one another without getting bitchy. And when they want to, they can cooperate on teams or in packs to play games or hunt. Men take it for granted that they have to protect themselves and their stuff. They are capable of being caretakers. And when ugly and scary things start to happen, men know they have to get off their asses and go meet fire with fire. They are physically brave in a way that most women can't imagine. Without the fire wall of homophobia and dildo envy, straight men and butch dykes would bond with one another. We have a lot in common.

Traditional straight women (and a surprising number of postfeminist wenches) think that life is about finding a man who will take care of them. He is supposed to be responsible for picking up the check at dinner, keeping the car in good running order, providing a dwelling and maintaining it, feeding and clothing his wife and children, protecting them from danger, and being good in bed besides. Men are supposed to do all this in exchange for . . . what? Pussy? Give me a break. Nobody has sex that good.

At least, heterosexuals usually don't have sex that good,

because if women admit that they enjoy sex as much as men do, it loses its value as a bargaining chip. The dynamic has to be: you do this awful thing to me that only you enjoy, so in return I expect summer vacations in Europe, diamond rings, and my own car. Straight women sabotage their men. They say no when they mean yes, and yes when they mean no. They won't ask for what they want. If they get what they want, they won't admit it. If they want more, they won't say so. They won't talk about their own bodies in a clear way. They act as if they were revolted by men's bodies and fluids. A man who is too good in bed (remember, sensitive = wussy) or too adventurous (kinky = feminine) always runs the risk of being told he is less than truly masculine. If he wants a finger up his butt, that's it; in the divorce she'll take him for everything and tell all his friends he's a fairy.

Is it any wonder that paying $40 for a blow job in a parked car looks like a bargain to most men? Look what they're expected to pay for romantic love, an ongoing, committed relationship.

No, I don't want to sleep with straight women. Not even once. Not even for one day. There are a few dykes I know who would be curious enough to tumble into bed with me, and certainly some bisexual girls who are lots of fun. But let's remember, on this day I am being male. I am no longer a woman who can come dozens of times in one day. I have two or three orgasms in me, if I'm lucky. So I have to prioritize. I have to figure out what I want the most, and do that first.

I have to admit that I would probably head straight for the baths and see what it is like to prowl after hungry gay-boy butt. Let's assume that if I were a man, I would look like one of my brothers. The one whose baby pictures often got mixed up with my own. So I would be short and stocky, with a thick single eyebrow. Physically, I would be very strong, with dark brown hair that was just a little curly, and a thick beard the same color. I'd have a few gray hairs, just enough to look as if I'd been around and done it all. No bald spots, which is too bad, because I think receding hairlines are pretty fucking sexy. My body wouldn't be very hairy, which is fine if you have enough muscle. I would have a deep voice and a quick mind. If annoyed, I would be prone to talking mean. But I would have a long fuse. It would take a lot to piss me off. Once I got mad, though, I would level whatever had enraged me. Men in my family take violence seriously. It's a last resort, but when they have to use force they are not at all ambivalent. They are good at it.

Men in my family also like sex. They are not guilty about enjoying their own bodies, and women tend to follow them around and look available. I know what it is like to be the queer daughter of a man whose ideas of male and female, right and wrong, are extremely old-fashioned. My dad is secretly pleased that I'm a dyke, because it means there will never be another man in my life who is more important than he is. He is also baffled by it and ashamed of me. The verbal abuse and violence I took for being a tomboy and a butch teenager were awful, but they weren't nearly as scary as the beatings my brothers got every time they showed even a faint tinge of effeminacy. What would it be like to be the queer son of such a man? It has been fairly easy for me to reject the guilt and self-hatred that my parents tried to inculcate in me for being a dyke. It feels like a package of junk mail I don't want, so I just toss it in the trash. But I think it's different for queer boys. In this culture, it is easier for girls to grow up to be women than it is for boys to grow up to be men. The state of manliness is more important, so it has to be a struggle to achieve. Manhood is a precarious identity. There is an arduous training period with draconian punishments for failure. And one of your tests, as a boy-becoming-a-man, is to accept that punishment without wincing or complaining. You have to take it like a man, and you have to make that stoicism a part of your very bones. Women are expected to be born with the capacity to suffer without really acknowledging it or trying to escape. Our pain is taken for granted, while a boy's task is to render his own pain absolutely invisible.

The relationship between a boy and his father is more desperate than the relationship between a girl and her mother. I did not particularly want to grow up to be like my mother, but that simply meant I would grow up to be a different kind of woman, not a man. A boy can always fail and be not-a-man, a sissy, a fag, a queen, a queer. A girl. There is a greater sense of betrayal when a boy cannot become a man. His father's sense of masculinity is forfeited as well as his own. Dykes are seen as neuters. Gay boys are seen as being somehow female. We both get tortured for being different, but I think the gay boys are seen as the greater heretics.

It makes me wonder if I would have survived coming out as gay, if I had been male. I think I would have been an awfully butch fag. It would be my way of compensating for the slaps, punches, and taunts, my way of saying, "Fuck you, I am as much a man as you are, Dad. I just happen to prefer fucking other men to fucking women." But there would always be that core of doubt, an insecurity that would make me vulnerable to the criticism of others. So I would be vain. I would crave admiration. I would be a slave to my gymnasium. I would be promiscuous, because the praise or admiration of one man would never be enough to mend the heart broken by my father. I would be kind to the men I loved, but I would be wary of long-term attachments, because living with another man is so much more queer than simply getting a blow job or sticking your cock up a cute piece of ass. I would hear my father sneering, "What do you want to be, some big bodybuilder's little wifey?" and flush. But to shut up that caustic voice, I would do so many things that my father probably wanted to do and would not allow himself to enjoy. I would kiss other men with big sloppy kisses that would leave both our faces with mustache burn. I would piss on them and kiss them again. I would want to cover their faces with my cum and feel jets of their hot semen on my own body. I would be determined to extract every single possible thrill and delight from the virile bodies that I had paid such a terrible price to enjoy.

If I woke up with a cock and a man's body to go with it, I would be free of this emotional baggage. It would be as if I had been newborn in a world where there was no such thing as homophobia. I would get to see what it was like to be queer without knowing I was hated by the people who created me. That alone would be worth the angst of feeling my body taken over by strange hormones and an organ I've used only in fantasy.

It would be wonderful to simply walk out my front door as

a man. The fact that I had that gender would grant me all kinds of privileges. For one thing, I would no longer have the fear all women have in the back of their minds every time they leave the house. The world, of course, holds physical dangers for men as well as for women. But women are coached in the art of being afraid. It is drummed into us that we are always at risk of being raped, assaulted, killed just because we are women. I think I would gladly chop a few years off my life to know, for just one day, what it would feel like to live without the shadow of that terror.

San Francisco in 1996 is not the gay mecca it was in 1976. But there are still enough sex clubs and other gathering places to feed a lust for casual sex. I would want to go to the Eros Center, a large two-story club on Market Street that is clean and well-lit. It's not known for being particularly kinky, so I probably wouldn't stay long. But I would want the experience of sexual license and the sensuality of group nudity. I would want to feel my naked body brushing against other men's, would want to turn and cup their cocks and know (through whatever mysterious cocksucker's alchemy) who was going to kneel and take the other down his throat. And perhaps there would be some handsome man with a certain look in his eye, a lost look, a look that says, "Take me," which would inspire me to turn him over and bend him across my body and paddle his butt. But at the Eros Center, it's much more likely that I would have another kind of curiosity gratified, the curiosity about what it's like to stick my hard dick through a hole in the wall and feel some stranger suck me in. Or kneel to perform for others' pleasure. I imagine that for men, sexual need is both simpler and more intense. I would like to feel the directness of the masculine libido, how easy it is to know what you want and be satisfied.

Then I'd want to cruise the Eagle, which is the only thing that really passes for a leather bar South of Market anymore. It has an outdoor patio, and the door on the bathroom is chained open, to prevent anybody from having sex in private. The owners are pretty nervous about keeping their liquor license, so they break up anything that looks like it might draw down the wrath of the state alcoholic beverages commission. But I would want to be there anyway, even if no sexual opportunity immediately presented itself. Rubbing leather shoulders and looking other men in the eye. Ordering a drink and being given it with a smile.

Being a woman in this place is not much fun. Most of the men who go there are aware that there is a leatherdyke community. We've done so much AIDS fund-raising and taking care of our sick brothers that it's become politically incorrect to banish us completely. But the Eagle is still a boys' club. There's a big difference between being tolerated and being welcomed. And another big difference between being recognized as an inferior variation of the "leather lifestyle," and being a hot new stud who has the evening of a lifetime in his gift.

Then there's also the fact that I've been thrown out of the Eagle a couple or fifteen times for the high crime of doing S/M in an S/M establishment. Leatherdykes have bad reputations among gay leathermen because too often we play with knives, and our games get a little heavier than they like. It's disconcerting, when you think you are at the top of the more-masculine-than-thou food chain, to see somebody half your size inflict (or take) punishment that would send you howling out the door. For many men, black leather is a fetish in and of itself that does not imply an interest in bondage or pain. My gender is a convenient excuse not to play with me. The real reason is my enthusiasm with flogger and cane, my gift for verbal dissection, and my fondness for shiny sharp things. It takes more than facial hair and a pair of big balls to make a sadist of my ilk. The fact is, I scare the shit out of most leathermen. No, I am not a welcome visitor at the Eagle.

So I'd like to get cruised by some of the men who have bumped into me, stepped on me, or just ignored me. I'd like to blow cigar smoke in their faces and pinch their tits and spit in their faces and leave them all with huge roaring hard-ons when I took myself out the door to a seedier and pervier environment, someplace where S/M is not an abbreviation for "Stand and Model."

The place I have in mind used to be a hotel. Now it's an underground sex club. Very few people know about it. It doesn't advertise, for fear of being closed down by the cops. Nevertheless, on a Saturday night, it is packed full of men, roaming the hallways, looking for something to quiet their raging flesh. The doors have been taken off most of the rooms. A few rooms are full of mattresses, which invite cluster fucks or group J/O sessions. But most of the rooms are equipped with the severe furniture of sadomasochism: slings, crosses, padded bondage horses, dangling chains.

I would like to prowl through the crowd until I found

someone I fancied. If my female tastes are any indication, I would be looking for someone who was bigger and meaner than me. He should have a dark beard and white, white skin. Intelligent, sad eyes. If he's normally a top who is unable to suppress his masochistic streak on this particular evening, so much the better. Honey, come here, let me scratch that evil itch. Oh, and I want him on the hefty side. Skinny boys are zeroes on my peter meter. I want someone who will talk back to me, somebody who understands that sex is boring without a steady stream of heartfelt filth.

I will slide my hands over his chest, which should be bare, and barely touch his nipples, which will get hard. Then I will wrap my leather-clad hands around his throat and squeeze it while I stick my tongue into his mouth. I want him to be stooping to take my kiss, the change in his posture just a harbinger of how far he has yet to fall. And I want him breathless from the excitement of having his mouth raped and from the dangerous pressure on his carotid arteries.

A push is next, a push that will straighten him up and send him backward against a wall. There is something exciting about having the breath knocked out of you by collision with a solid object. And then there is the erotic confusion of being securely held up and in place, but also being trapped, by the wall behind you. It will be too early in the game for any bondage other than a hand pressed against his throat or my whole body leaning against his. Time for more kisses, these with some teeth. Time for licking and biting his nipples, unzipping his pants, squeezing his cock and making sure it welcomes me. Nearby there will be a room, and I will whisper in his ear, "Are you ready for me to take you into that room? Because once I get you in there, you won't be allowed to leave until you have satisfied me completely." He will say yes, or simply nod his head, or hold his tongue (silence is consent).

Then it is time to turn him around, pin his hands behind his back, and march him forward through a crowd of jealous and occasionally disapproving spectators. Those who want to watch will come after us. I will ignore them. They are not important. This man whose hands I have pinioned is important. He is a mission I have chosen to accept, but not an impossible one.

Past the threshold, I trip him and admire him sprawling, big man, so strong, healthy animal, led by his own appetites to do things that are not wise. The desire to be a dumb blond knows no gender. A secret part of all of us craves unconditional adoration, to receive the ardent attention of a mysterious stranger simply because we are beautiful. Dominance and submission is about singling someone out for worship as much as it is about physical restraint or pain. There's nothing really stupid about most dumb blonds, or this brunet who has chosen to make himself the object of my hunt. By the end of this evening, he will be wiser than he is now.

"Strip," I tell him, and when he tries to get up to do it, I kick him back down. "Undress on your knees," I suggest, and he takes it for an order. You learn so much from new conquests by watching how they fulfill this requirement. Are they in a hurry? Do they have the coquetry to turn the exercise into a subtle one of flirtation and display, hesitation and then yielding? Are they ashamed? Or have they already left their bodies far behind? And what do they do with the protective covering they have removed? Do they leave it crumpled in a heap? That bodes ill. I think boys should clean up after themselves. His mother is hardly going to creep in here and silently remove his garments for laundering. And I don't want to trip over the detritus of his other life.

Because I like him and he's given me a massive boner, I will let him lick my boots. This is a promise that after suffering, there will be pleasure. Great pleasure. But he has to earn it first, I tell him, and he agrees. He understands quite well the concept that you must work to deserve your reward. It is, in some ways, the essence of what makes him a man. And I am happy to use this good-boy work ethic for my own nefarious purposes. He has been waiting all his life for a stronger man to tell him to do a difficult job, and then pet him when he succeeds. I am such a badass daddy that I will do that: I will tell him he's a good boy when he sucks my cock and offers me his ass. If you do not understand how deep the injuries are that can be healed by this treatment, you have never been a queer boy who was beaten in the schoolyard for liking other boys too much.

With broad leather wrist cuffs padded with sheepskin, I fasten him face first to the cross. His ankles will be shackled as well, to prevent kicking. With thin rope I will bind his cock so that he cannot shoot without being released from its embrace, and I extend the bondage into a harness that encircles his waist and holds a butt plug in place. Let him have no doubt while he is being flogged how he will eventually serve me. The plug will remind him that he is too valuable to be destroyed, that he has sweeter uses than to swing at the end of my whips.

But that is slight comfort when leather lashes contact skin. Do you think I will beat him as a proxy for all the abominable things men have done to women? Do you think I will make him a scapegoat, the butt of my rage? I will not. If I am a man, this man becomes my brother. I do not flog him to punish him for being queer or to shame him for being the lesser man. My whips are instruments of praise and redemption, not brutality or torture. I will whip him as an exorcism. I will beat shame off his shoulders and banish it from the tight cheeks of his ass. I will open up his heart and set him free to weep. I will imprison him in his own flesh and force him to accept his own body; then I will set him free from the boundary of his own skin and let him fly. And then I will call him home and let him bless my armpit with his tongue, my face with his kisses, while our cocks meet and precum mingles.

I know how to do this. Like all the most important skills I possess, it transcends gender. Each whip I have is like a different language, a unique tongue I can speak to him to teach him a new catechism, a litany that says, What men do to please one another sexually is sacred and good. It takes a while, and by the time I am done my muscles are burning. Both of us are tired. But not too tired to take our reward.

I unchain him and he falls (no, soars) to my feet and takes me with his lips, his tongue, his throat. We share the forbidden knowledge that men everywhere have shared, often at enormous cost: our bodies fit together thus, and so, and oh, oh, oh, it's good. Cock and ball bondage has to be removed. The butt plug falls out, having done its job. He is well spread. Then I put him on his back on the floor and take him up the ass, almost too impatient to grease us both up, and I pound him as if I could force all of myself into his body. Men are not supposed to do this, to share cum with one another. Our cum is supposed to be dirty. It is supposed to be used only for making babies. But I wrap my fist around his cock and we come together, sliding against each other in a pool of sweat and semen that bathes away frustration and doubt.

Misogyny is not the only cause of rape or other crimes against women. So much male violence springs from self-hatred. When men share cum with one another, they are breaking, in the most deep and fundamental way possible, the taboos that enforce patriarchal sex roles and mandatory heterosexuality. Because this is my fantasy, my day to do all the things I would do if I were a man, I do not reach for a rubber before I fuck the handsome stud who has given me his pain and submission and blessed me with his tears. In my fantasy, at least, it is safe for men to baptize one another, take communion from one another, join together to make a new religion that makes pleasure a sacrament and eschews hatred of the body.

🖫

The next day, when I wake up in my own body again, I think I will feel two things: disappointment and anger. Anger at losing the size, strength, and privileges that make men swagger down the street. Anger at losing access to the secret world where men stick their tongues in one another's mouths and their hands in one another's jeans. And disappointment at being back in a world where men and women might as well be members of different species or alien races speaking different languages, so little do we know of each other's history and hopes for the future. Someday it will not be this way. And that is why I will still be here tomorrow, working impossibly hard to get both men and women to look at the walls we have built around ourselves and wonder what might be on the other side, and also to realize that "men" and "women" are only two of the ways that human beings can experience gender and sexuality.

There are always more than two choices. Always. Always. Always.

In my dreams, I have a dick. Not in all of them, only in the good ones. Not just for a day, but for always.

The first time I dreamed of having a dick, I was seven. I was standing in the bathroom wearing a pair of big white boxer shorts, and attached to my body was a new organ full of wonderful sensation. The sensuality of the dream was marred only slightly by the fact that I was Tom Bosley of *Happy Days*.

I've always known I was queer, but saying "I'm not a lesbian, I'm a fag in a female body" doesn't help matters a great deal in high school, so I stayed at home nights dreaming, and eventually writing, about the torrid sex lives of gay boys. In 1995, Kate Bornstein's book *Gender Outlaw* finally clued me in to the liberating term "non-operative transsexual."

A dick for a day? I would spend the day worshiping it, as dick possessors tend to do, and letting it do the thinking, as dicks will. I would give it over to the mouths and hands and assholes of as many tantalizing men as I could get my hands on. I would be the worst nelly slut you ever saw. And, for once in my life, I would mourn the coming of night.

Swollen Tide

GINU KAMANI

Behind the house stood five acres of cool orchard, thick with
mango and guava trees. Every third day Ramu the gardener
opened the taps and let the water flood the channels. Every
tree was dammed in by a mud wall. Through a small opening the water rushed in and surrounded the trunk. Ramu
walked ankle deep through the cold mud, making sure that
the dams remained unbroken. The water racing between his
toes was as delicious as shaved ice, and Ramu fought back
the urge to gulp it down in mouthfuls. Away from the shaded
orchard the desert heat bleached the landscape, devoid of all
life except a few buzzing insects.

That day there were women in the orchard, enclosing the
still-hard guavas in protective netting, tying the bags quickly,
tucking and retucking their heavily embroidered skirts between their legs. Ramu could hear the women talking quietly
as they laced up each fruit with nimble fingers. The women

stepped without looking, crushing the walls of the dams. Ramu hurried toward them and they turned to him, laughing.

"Oh, Ramu, in trouble again, eh? Keep your head clear, you hear? Watch your step around Memsahib!" Ramu reshaped the dams and the women moved on. "Ssssss!" Their long sibilant breaths released between pleasurably clenched teeth. "Sssss!" Their feet sank deep into the cool mud, dredging the earth.

Ramu was looking for Omi. Every day he made his rounds energetically, hoping to catch a glimpse of her. He was not allowed into the house except when summoned by Memsahib; after all, his job was as a gardener. He prayed every day for a summons. Once, just once, he had seen Omi inside the house, and from then on he fretted every day until he saw her. She had been playing with the children, twirling around with her mirrored skirt flying higher and higher, while the youngsters watched from below. The sight of her bare thighs made his throat constrict with fear. He tried to signal to her but she was laughing aloud, eyes closed. Finally Ramu kicked over a brass vase and the deafening clang brought them running. With one piercing look from him Omi understood his terror. Dazed by her carelessness, Ramu remained rooted to the spot until Memsahib shouted for him again.

When Memsahib called for him, he walked around the orchard and past the stable of Highness, the mare, past the doghouse of the high-pitched Honey, who was always tied in front. In the back of the house he was usually accosted by the lonely cook, who dragged him into the servants' room to smoke a *bidi* and play a quick hand of cards. This man had come from Bombay. He spoke very little Hindi and no Rajasthani, so Ramu and he communicated mostly with gestures and laughter. The cook chewed on tobacco mixed with lime paste. He would spit over the steps onto the lawn, even when Memsahib was around. She never said a word. According to her, he was the only man in Rajasthan who could prepare Gujarati food to her liking, and the cook knew it well. After extinguishing the leaf cigarette Ramu would point to the house and shrug. The cook would smile and nod and push the pack under his pillow. Ramu would wipe his feet thoroughly on the coir mat and enter the main house.

Memsahib could be heard loud and clear and it was usually easy to find her. Recently, she had been in the storeroom, off the kitchen. Ramu was headed in the direction of her voice when out of the corner of his eye he saw a peacock alight on the lawn. He froze, then moved cautiously toward the preening bird, its head tucked under one wing. On seeing him, the peacock jerked upright, wing held high. Ramu and the bird stared at each other. It was the middle of the day, and peacocks only ever flew onto the cool lawns at dawn and twilight. Ramu could almost feel the bird's delight as it repeatedly gripped the moist grass, soaking in the lushness, darting moisture up its legs. The peacock turned around with delicate steps until it faced away from the house. Then it lay down on its side, neck retracting with every movement. Ramu trembled with excitement to see the mighty bird hugging the ground like an electric flowering bush. It reminded him of Omi.

Suddenly overhead a vulture came swooping toward the

peacock, which broke into a run and lumbered screaming into the air, pendulously flapping its way to the roof. The vulture circled away. Memsahib was watching Ramu from the kitchen. He ran around to the back to wipe his wet feet once again before presenting himself for work.

⚛

Tired of running around the property to locate Omi, Ramu marked off a large plot of earth, well hidden among the thickets, which became the children's playground. There they built castles and moats, dug for worms and snakes, planted beans, peas, or any other seed that sent up tall shoots overnight. And there they stationed Omi to help them, allowing Ramu to keep an eye on her.

In the hot season, the air was so dry that just hours after the channels had run full, the earth of the orchard cracked again. On those days, the children would have Omi fill water in brass pots and carry it out to their playground. Omi waited until the moats and wells were dug, then hefted the brass pots with sure aim. Ramu loved to watch her work. Omi was Devi, the great goddess whose calm exterior hid her fiery interior. Ramu loved the children because they loved Omi like their own mother, without calling attention to her extraordinary ways.

The children always played together, digging or building side by side. They spoke in their made-up language, but they also spoke some Hindi, so Ramu could understand them. If he stopped for a few minutes to smoke his *bidi*, he would tell the children stories of Devi and the temples he had visited since childhood. But Ramu spoke only Rajasthani, so they didn't understand most of what he said. Of all the servants only Omi spoke enough Hindi to talk to the children. Memsahib had called for a Hindi-speaking woman for the house, and ever since then Omi had stayed.

Omi's job was to care for the children and the pets. She worked separately from the other villagers, who labored outdoors. Memsahib especially wanted Gujarati spoken to the animals, so Omi learned a few words with which to coax the animals to eat, or take their walks, or perform tricks. She was the only villager allowed through the front entrance of this big house which the laborers were convinced was full of strange goings-on: Memsahib always hidden away somewhere, locked inside her office, bedroom, storeroom; voices echoing from all sides so one couldn't tell where they came from.

But to Omi, the house was a serene palace to which the peacocks flocked, where even dogs and horses were treated like kings. When Omi spoke like that, believing things that no other villagers did, Ramu struggled with all his old fears. But fearing the spirit of the Devi in her, he could not openly contradict her. And just like the Devis who bided their time patiently in their big, beautiful temples, this Devi also needed a beautiful house in which to recuperate before the inevitable return of danger.

⚭

Ramu went about his rounds through the dense trees, shoring up dams, widening the channels. The icy mud invigorated his tired bones. Suddenly the children came splashing through the water, the boy chasing after his sister and flipping up her dress, shouting: "Peep show! Peep show!" Ramu laughed and laughed as the two ran around the trees. "Stop it!" the girl hissed, out of breath. The boy halted, red-faced and panting. Immediately the gardener sensed that something was wrong: the children were best friends, and Ramu had never seen them fight.

Hearing the sounds of the children, the women came closer to pick the ripe guavas. They threw teasing comments at the children, which neither understood. The boy lunged at a woman, throwing her thick skirt into the air and exposing the backs of her thighs. The bewildered woman slapped the ballooning material down and her shouting companions pinned the boy's hands behind his back. He struggled for a bit, but was too tired to fight. The girl ran off toward the house, and the boy followed.

As Ramu watched the agitated boy dissolve into the shimmering heat, he was reminded of something. Perhaps it was how, years earlier, he and his friends would ride their bicycles along the dirt paths traveled by village women who were returning home staggering under bundles of firewood. Using their long, curved herding staffs the men would hook the swishing skirt hems, flipping the material straight up so that it snagged high and taut on the kindling, exposing the women from waist to foot. The women would drop their loads in horror, scattering sticks everywhere, cursing the laughing men who wobbled and circled at a distance, barely keeping their balance.

That afternoon, Memsahib sent for Ramu. Ramu was still troubled from the morning's events. He made a quick round of the grounds, looking for Omi; he searched in the houses of the horse and the dog, with no luck. He raced past the servants' room and through the kitchen, then slowed down as he approached the bedrooms. He turned the corner and almost ran into the girl, who was watching her brother as he hopped back and forth, face twisted with pain as Memsahib hit him with knitting needles, whipping him around the knees and calves and ankles. The needles were bent out of shape, making Memsahib bend lower and lower until she herself was bowing to the ground. The only sounds were of the swiftly moving needles humming through the air and landing on tender skin. Memsahib finally threw down the needles, and the boy fell back, gritting his teeth in pain. "What do you want?" Memsahib snapped at Ramu. He saluted her, stepped back, and turned away. This was not the time to remind her of the summons.

Right afterward, the children ran outside and once again the malicious game of peep show caused the boy to chase after his sister and lift her dress every other minute. The girl screamed and cried. Memsahib came dashing out of the house, almost tripping as she jumped from the verandah to the lawn. She caught the two children firmly; with one hand she pulled up her daughter's dress, and with the other she gripped her son's shoulder, shouting at him to *look, look, look, to his heart's content.* The boy trembled with fear. His eyes darted from his sister to his mother's face, back and forth, as she shouted at him to keep *peep-peep-peeping, enough for one whole lifetime!*

🏵

Ramu searched again for Omi in the houses of the animals. The channels must have been spilling over by now with the taps still running. The women might even have mashed all the dams with their feet, just to keep him working longer. In the house of the dog, many bowls of dal and vegetables and rice had been laid out, just like Memsahib's lunch. For the horse there was lots of new hay, and sweet balls of sesame mixed with jaggery. Ramu's forehead was hot from worrying, and his heart grew cramped in his chest. Usually when he went in search of Omi, his brain would empty and his heart would swell. He might cool her legs with the wet mud, or fill her skirt with green mangoes. But sooner or later with Omi, try as he might to protect her, something was bound to go wrong.

The gardener and the children continued searching for Omi. The horse was feeding on hay, Honey was sleeping, satiated: Omi had come and gone. The children were losing interest and they dragged their feet, kicking soft cold mud at each other's legs. Omi did that sometimes to cool off—dipping her hands into an irrigation channel and scooping up the wet earth, lathering the mud over her dry calves. Often she rubbed upward over her legs, reaching to her abdomen, then lay down in the shade to rest. In that fertile layer of mud, with the nourishing warmth of her skin underneath, anything could grow. Sometimes Ramu threw guava seeds on her mud-caked limbs, imagining how they'd sprout into a curtain of green tendrils.

He looked on all sides but didn't see her. "Why not ask the cook?" thought Ramu. The door to the cook's room was shut. Ramu put his ear to the door, wondering whether he was asleep, then saw smoke curling from under the door and pushed it open. The cook was hidden behind his arm-wrapped legs, a forgotten *bidi* hanging from the corner of his mouth. Next to him, tucked under him, was his rifle. The same rifle he shot with in the Indian army, defending the country against enemies. Ramu quickly snatched the rifle and tossed it onto the shelf out of harm's way. Mad cook! Could he have pointed his gun at Omi?

The cook appeared to be drugged. He rasped in a voice not his own: "I fought the war in China, I fought the war in Pakistan, but never, never have I seen anything like this woman, never . . . !"

"Where is she?" Ramu shook him roughly, but the fear in the cook's eyes made it clear that he did not know.

They marched to the front of the house. Outside the gates they heard a commotion. Ramu and the children ran down the driveway and pushed through the crowd. Lying in the dirt was Omi. "She's doing it again," whispered the boy, hiding behind his sister's back. The girl cursed in anger and dragged her brother away.

Omi sprawled in the street asleep, her legs wide open, her skirt bunched up. Her still figure was encircled by a jostling crowd, who pushed first one way and then the next, jockeying for position in front of her marigold-strewn maidenhead, then averting their eyes with howls of alarm that triggered a violent pulsation through the crowd.

Hundreds of people blocked the street. The watchman trembled with shame, wondering what to do. The evening light was fading, and suddenly Sahib's car was honking its way through the crowd. Sahib stepped out of the car, took one look at Omi, and fell back onto his seat. When he stood up again, he was shaking. "Who is this madwoman?" he shouted. "Which sisterfucker has thrown her in front of my house?"

The crowd quieted down. Those who knew felt sorry for him, and those who didn't yet know felt sorry that a man of such standing couldn't show more devotion. Sahib lashed out with his cane, forcing the crowd back. "Why are you here? Get out of the street. Go back to your homes!" He spotted Ramu by the gate. "Eh Ramu! Tell these wretched fools to get away."

"Sahib." Ramu bowed respectfully. "They have come for pilgrimage, Sahib. They cannot leave until they have worshiped Devi and received blessings. Sahib, please, you must turn the car around and come to the back. I will open the gate—"

"What Devi?" Sahib was trembling with rage. "What madness are you talking about! Isn't this woman my servant? She will do as I say." He lifted his cane to strike.

The panicked crowd snapped together like an accordion, lifting up the body of the Sahib and flinging him onto the periphery. The bodies parted and Ramu came forward. A fistful of blazing marigolds was thrust into his hand. He knelt before the shrine of Omi. She moved in her sleep and her legs widened. He stared at the expanse of skin stretching from knees to hips. He quickly touched his palms to the dense matting of Omi's womb, clasped his hands reverentially, then smoothed the palms over his head and chest. "O Lord," prayed Ramu, "how long must my woman suffer this fate?"

Omi sighed sharply. The rapid fluttering of her abdomen gently dislodged the offerings of orange petals, permitting the ghostly miracle to be fully revealed. The crowd groaned in agony. Plainly visible for all to see was the rigid straining organ of a newborn male, so milky translucent on Omi's dark skin, so pure and innocent between her rounded feminine thighs that it could be mistaken for a flower. A lingam born erect into the world was a lingam of Shiva, a manifestation of power and love. Once a year when the faraway oceans swelled and the moon filled to bursting and the villagers finally rested on their hard-won harvest, Omi surrendered herself to rebirthing the organ that fused her in divine union, like Shiva-Parvati, Shiva-Shakti, like Gauri-Shankar, Linga-Yoni.

Ramu touched his forehead to the ground in respect. He heard Sahib's car move forward, honking and pushing through the resistant crowd. The watchman threw open the gate, then stood in stiff salute as the car raced through. The gate clanged shut. The finality of steel on steel snapped the crowd out of its reverie. A brief shower of coins rained down on Ramu's head, knocking together like sonorous marbles. The devout paid their final respects and then were gone.

As he gathered up the money, Ramu finally heard the gushing sounds of water that had overrun the grounds, that swirled around him now in sudden streams. The cold shock of the flood invigorated him and he scooped handfuls onto his face. He shifted Omi onto his lap, then waited for the miracle to blossom. With the rapidity only barren desert can enforce, seedlings lying dormant sprang up through the deepening pools, shooting up in abandon, enveloping man-woman in new green life. Touching his parched lips to this unrepentant tide, Ramu gave thanks to the swollen lingam and raised Omi high up to the silvery sky.

bidi: hand-rolled leaf cigarette
jaggery: residue from sugar refining, like molasses
linga, lingam: phallus
yoni: female genitals
Shiva: god of creation and destruction
Parvati: wife of Shiva
Shakti: active feminine principle of the cosmos
Shankar: an epithet of Shiva
Gauri: an epithet of Parvati

Marilyn Monroe Dreams of Growing Her Own Penis Under Roots of Trees

LYN LIFSHIN

It's been 33 years she
thinks, lying back under
damp ivy, long enough
for other movers and
shakers to do what
had to be done.
Being dead's a little
like being in a
bomb shelter. Cozy she
thinks and peace and
quiet were enough
for so long. Only now,
she thinks of a bone
that wasn't her hip or
wrist, wasn't her
ankles on a grate

mosquitoes clawed as
they blew air up under
her red dress, even
her lips down there
going rosy. She knows
how long it's been
since she's had more
than enough other
flesh wedged up inside
them close as a Siamese
twin but never as
comforting, never there
just for her long enough.
She feels the leaves
mulch her toes, her
gray hair cradling her
bones, a better pillow
than a man who'll roll away,
keep her awake snoring.
For a year she dreamt of
another set of boobs
she'd hip hop all night
with, watching men drool.
What a relief to be out
with a joined twin, on
her own but not lonely,
someone who'd be there
not only at the moment
of death, but even after. She
imagines something moving

between her thighs that
isn't her own hand, in its
bracelet of need but a
bud, a bloom, a flesh lily
she won't have to shove what's
left of her legs for, that
can fill her up, moving gently,
as if she was a virgin (and
she might as well have been
it's been so long),
knowing exactly what she
wants and where to move it,
linked to her heart,
there for as long
as she needs it, oozing
crystals she's heard
are the rage and then
like a kitten embryo
that won't be born
and leave the mother's
fur or make a mess
or claw or stake its
own territory, be
resorbed back into
her blood maybe to
swell and bloom again
under a red hunger moon

Academic Figure Study I

AMY JENKINS

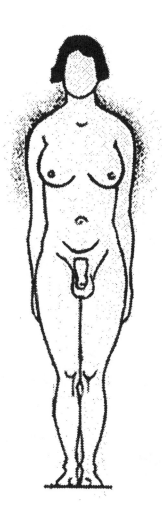

Amy's Inches

AMY JENKINS

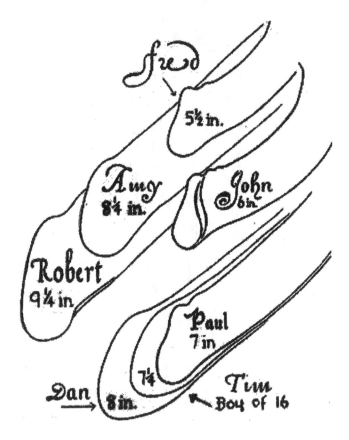

Cheap Revenge

INEZ BARANAY

Just before midnight I'd enter the girls-only space as a man disguised as a woman and leave it as me. This was not easy to explain. I remembered what Alison had told me only the night before.

"Do you know what I mean? Something you wanted so badly—you finally get it—it doesn't mean the same."

Alison was finishing the story of her answered prayer. "By the time this call came, I didn't care."

"The tragedy of the wish come true."

We paid our bill and stepped out into the buzzy trashed night of Oxford Street.

"Well I'm glad we saw it anyway," we said of the stupid movie. "And that was good," we said of the restaurant we'd just tried, enjoying some beers with our Mexican food and babbling our way through several intense topics of conversation: her work, my work, the world. "And tomorrow then, dearest," we said, kissing, "tomorrow night."

We had a regular date to go dancing at Puta Scandalosa: girls' night, Sundays at Roget's just down the road. We'd done it twice and were going to do it forever.

She got into her car and I turned to walk home. Consumers of culture were milling at nightclub entrances, restaurants were closing, and substance-enhanced people were hailing taxis. It was late enough to arrive at the dance party at the showground that night.

I was going home to sleep, for now the walk through Darlinghurst all of my thrill. Tomorrow night around this hour I'd be out. I hadn't seen much of Ali for ages—sometimes career and travel steal time—but now we were both "around," as we said, "for now." Keeping late hours and invigorated by some novel gratitude: alive, well, fit; you didn't take it for granted these days that we still were up to it, going dancing, our hips bumped by girls so young we were never like that.

🍄

I struggled to wake up. I was on my sofa. When I'd come home I must have passed out immediately. I felt most peculiar and thought immediately of food poisoning. It wasn't just nausea, or not even nausea at all exactly. More a drugged, half-dreaming sensation that wouldn't go away, even as I pinched myself and reached for my glass of water. It *was* nausea, actually.

It was as if I couldn't get back into my body as I woke— or came to. But also I was very much in my body, which felt violently disturbed, or perhaps disturbingly violent. I struggled to recognize myself; my hands flew to the cushiony solace of my breast; horror infested mystification. I really did not seem to be asleep.

I stood and nearly keeled over with the unfamiliar center of gravity. The fact of a metamorphosis sank into my apprehension.

It was three A.M. and I was coming out of shock. My body had transformed, or I had transmuted, and though somehow I knew I was still I, I was no longer I. How could I be?

Did this mean, though, that I was now a man? If a man is a person with a penis. I looked at it from every angle, using mirrors. I had always found my cunt entirely beautiful—a flower, a seashell, sweet-talking lips. This new set of apparatus aroused a different fascination, ambivalent, tinged with pride and protectiveness. My horror dissolved in my curious attention to the sensations of my mind and the responses of my new body.

As I stroked my dick—I think it was a dick at this point, rather than a penis or a cock—as if to soothe my puzzlement away, it responded with a heated swelling. As a sensation for my hand this was not entirely unfamiliar, and yet its own commanding sensation was original. Getting hard didn't feel quite the same as getting wet, I didn't think, but it was odd that I was no longer sure. Certainly I experienced an inner arousal pushed out, for a moment, anyway, until it seemed too peculiar to think it could be otherwise.

Sticky with saliva, the dick throbbed—but then felt

cold and lifeless, for my puerile action suddenly seemed so pathetic I was unable to continue. The sense of being watched had become unnerving, even though the watcher was me.

✿

A man I knew who liked to wear dresses said he enjoyed how they made him feel: more elegant, more alert to his body. I had always liked men in frocks. I'd always liked women in butch apparel, especially if subverted by some lace or lipstick. Which I would forgo, now, as I was already sufficiently deconstructed. I decided on the jeans, T-shirt, sweatshirt, boots. An imitation for which there is no original.

I had enjoyed the remnants of male association previously held by this attire. As these supposedly degendered items had been worn by the woman I was, I now suspected them of being imbued with an aura of the female, lending an androgynous cast to my otherwise masculine new appearance. This could not be a bad thing.

I surveyed my arsenal of moisturizers with bemusement and had an odd swift wish for a toolbox: spanners, screwdrivers, wrenches—whatever they were.

The clothes fit, but not in quite the same way. I took off the sweatshirt, as I no longer felt the cold. I was disappointed that I had not grown any taller.

✿

I live in this part of town because it's the part that never closes. But at four A.M. the streets have quieted. And look who I see, as if I'd been looking for her.

We used to nod a vague, barely acknowledged recognition of each other back when I used to work the graveyard shift subediting at the paper. I'd be on my way home around now, and often stop right here for a last cappuccino before turning in.

Although she was paid for her appearances in *Woman's Day* and on *60 Minutes*, she had found that five-minute fame doesn't keep you in hormones and body wax, and was working the same old beat.

She doesn't recognize me now. Zanni the Tranni leans into her doorway and bends one knee to prop her foot on the wall behind her. As I approach she waves a sodden cigarette at me. "Got a light, love?" she inquires in a husky voice ravaged by irony.

"Don't smoke," I say, but I've stopped.

"No vices, eh?"—winking as she puts the cigarette back into the pocket of her pink jacket. She whispers then— "Short time, long time, hand job, blow job, full strip, Visa, Amex."

I follow her. Inside the doorway rickety steps lead to the demesne of her disclosures. It is an area lovingly designed in the hot pink, tigerskin patterns, and amber prints of olden-days TV stars.

"All I want to do is talk."

"Oh, shit." She shrugs with weary tolerance. "Cost you double." She sits heavily atop the creaking bed. "Any specific topic of converzazionay?" Her head tilts to one side in a gesture of attempted coquetry; it comes out as mild contempt.

"You were saving for an operation," I begin.

She assents with a gracious inclination of her bewigged head, apparently not displeased to be recalled to her tabloid moment.

"Just tell me something. Why did you want it off?"

She looks at me with patience and disdain. "How would you like to be a woman with a dick?"

She has the tits and the smooth face that I don't—not any longer or not for the moment. "That's just it," I begin, and fall silent.

"I don't guarantee satisfaction," she answers my silence. "I only do what I've been asked. Talk is a two-to-tango thing." She crosses her thick legs, displaying broad knobbly feet in green satin platform shoes. "How much do you think it costs to get these shoes custom made?" she inquires bitterly. "People who inhabit their assigned gender don't know how lucky they are."

Her practiced sensitivity overcomes her self-absorption. "Why so glum?" she observes with momentary though gracious focus. "You seem all man to me, or man enough. I'm almost tempted to throw in a favor, but a deal's a deal. So what's up? Speak to me, darling. Many disparate desires dwell in dicks. You like to wear a frilly silken cami next to your hairy chest, nothing wrong with that, sweetheart."

"What if I don't want my dick?" I inquire, uneasy, for perhaps Zanni and I aren't in quite the same boat, and maybe not the same sea. Or what?

"It'd be a waste," she says flirtatiously, looking me up and down and up, batting her thick nylon eyelashes. Evidently she is unmoved by my peculiarity.

"Am I a man?" I implore.

She flares. "Youse make me sick, you think every one of us is bloody Tiresias with all the answers, youse all think sex has the answer to it all. Your time's up." She shows me the door.

I don't move.

"But wait—what if I know more about being a woman? Is knowledge of yourself as a woman erased in a man's body?"

She starts shoving. I resist. "Wait," I say. "Then what is a woman? You said you'd always been a woman—before the operation."

She picks me up in her strong though smooth-skinned arms.

"No, wait," I implore, gasping at the fumes of her scent. "Is sexual inscription a rewriting of an ontologically prior differentiation?"

She staggers with me to the landing.

"I know gender has a fluid range of possibilities. . . ." I plead.

She throws me down the stairs.

⚘

What am I now? Shy, good with cars, keen to arm-wrestle in pubs? Should I turn on the TV for one of those ball games? I go to the computer to see if I suddenly want to tinker with the programs. Maybe I could call my publisher at his house—fuck what time it is, I could get really assertive here, or at least arrange a game of golf.

Yeah, what about all that male privilege I've always been

angry about? Here was my chance to work it. I had the dick; that was all I needed. We'd always said so.

Hey, I'm not that kind of man. I'm unfettered by conditioning; my desire to get in touch with my feelings cancels out my need to find some guy I could beat at something. I need some understanding.

🐾

A dirty dawn light seeped into the café. It was always open and served coffee that blew your head off. The women didn't look as if they'd been partying all night. They looked as if they were between college lectures. Anything's possible in the city. I didn't look away; they couldn't make me. They were probably attracted to me, my cuts and bruises signaling an atavistic manly appeal: a warrior, a tough guy, walking the line.

I didn't realize I was staring. The three women glanced at me, leaned toward one another, muttered, glanced again. I had been staring. Why were they so offended? Think hard, try to remember. Why weren't they flattered?

"Ignore him," one said, loud enough for me to hear.

That was me at a younger age, turning my back—what a naïve tactic. "Never turn your back, honey," I thought now. "We're all beasts, and backs are for jumping."

"Confront him," said the other, pushing back her chair.

Uh-oh, another former self, acting as if her integrity required a show of umbrage and confrontation. And then she'd wonder why I'm convinced she's interested.

"Maybe," pleaded Three, tugging at Two's jacket as she rose, "we could ask, explain . . ."

I saw myself, younger still, believing all would be understood between fellow human beings of goodwill. Certain she could conciliate, sure she could soothe. My heart ached, I had been all of them once. "Give it up, girls," I thought. "There are no victories."

I leaned toward them. " 'Scuse me ladies, I can't help noticing . . ."

"Can't help . . . ! take no responsibility . . . *women* to you . . ." they mutter, letting me hear but not quite addressing me.

"You don't know me!" I was startled and hurt. How could they dislike me already? "If you don't want to talk to me, why do you look so pretty?"

"Not for your benefit," Two snarled.

It took me a moment to identify the discomfort of a growing erection tightening my jeans. Oh, gross, how inappropriate. Here I was all brotherly protectiveness and sisterly empathy, and here was a hard-on. My feeling for this rightfully resentful young woman was not lustful, I swear. The body has a mind of its own.

"Can't you see we're not here to talk to you?" Three suggested in a tone I guess I can't call patronizing.

"Just one question," I said, sounding very reasonable. "We're all human beings, aren't we? Is 'man' what I am or what I do?"

Reasonable did not impress.

One growled, "A man typically turns to women for attention to questions of emotion and identity." Like I was an exhibit, the evidence. So much for ignoring me. Just like me in those days when I had the theory.

Three declared with sorrowful insightfulness, "It's a

*man*ipulative ploy to engage us; he isn't interested, look at him—only into himself."

Two said, choking with anger, "I'd like to show him, show 'em all—oh, if only I had a dick for a day."

"Yeah!" went the others. "Yeah."

I reeled with revelation. "Only by becoming anatomically male do you stop hating men," I said excitedly. "That's what that wish is about, not some cheap revenge fantasy!"

"Jesus . . ." and they pushed back their chairs and flung themselves out of there.

⚭

Wasn't there a story where a siren changed men into swine? I see them, a bunch of startled pigs hurtling down an ancient Greek hillside. Homer, wasn't it? These transmogrifications were always a punishment or a test.

Or a way for a sly god to fuck some maiden: they turn into swans, bulls—some creature more irresistible than a man.

But this is a New Age era and there are no outside gods, only your own powerful choices.

I hadn't been the kind of girl I'd been brought up to be, and didn't grow into the kind of woman. Plus, I was responsible for the current widespread cultural confusions about sexuality, gender, and identity. In the sense that in the careful patterns of Chaos it might be my own personal contribution to the entire ecological totality of it all, that was one of those last-straw things, like a single beat of a butterfly wing that can cause derangement. More theory. As for practice, well. I confess I had not slept with anyone, man or woman, for—oh, never mind. I forget. Ages. Dating straight and gay men and women but never doing sex, I'd turned into that trendy cliché, the queer heterosexual. Not that I was, on that 1-to-6 scale they used to have, entirely het. I figured I was only expressing some of the complex affections, attractions, and restraints that were appropriate for now. The trajectory of my life had, along the line, disqualified me from both monogamous couples modeled on marriage and casual promiscuity. In my fantasy, without boring you with particulars, I was bi, gay, multi, omni, and equipped with selected accoutrements and accessories out of those tasteful pastel catalogs they advertise in women's magazines. How could I claim none of this was my actual experience? Imagination is experience, and experience is knowledge. Didn't I think so?

Did that make me a man?

☙

"You're not going to believe what I'm about to tell you," I begin when she picks up the phone.

"Who is this?" she asks.

"It's me—Inez. Well . . ."

"You sound strange; are you sick? You're not piking out of tonight? It's keeping me working all day."

It was a Sunday, but an independent film producer has no day of rest.

"I do want to go tonight. . . . Something strange has happened to me." I did not know how I'd ever imagined for the tiniest second that I could even begin to tell. "Ali," I said, "they don't let men into tonight, do they?"

"Did you want to ask someone?" she says, sounding disappointed. "No, they don't. Can I call you back? I've got London on the other line."

"Alison, what's happened—" I begin, but only in my head do I form the words *is so weird I don't know where to start.* "Hey, I'll try and explain tonight."

TRACY SONDERN

I'd pee all over the bathroom, the walls, the floor—every-where. Then I'd make my four brothers clean up, just like I always had to do after them.

Shhhhh

TRICIA WARDEN

I was dreaming about the librarian. The librarian is this de-
mure brunette who runs the rare book section in the public
library of my mind. She tells me to empty my pockets and es-
corts me quietly into some musty catacomb where she asks
me if I've ever kissed a woman before. I say yeah, wondering
what she's getting at. Then I spy a glowing red telephone on
an antique phone stand. I think she must use this phone to
call the parents of wanton lesbians and bisexuals to out them.
My stomach churns as she bypasses it completely and looks
at me dead on with this line, "Are you sure?" I don't say anything. She comes so close to me that my heart almost rips out
of my chest like a fist eager to punch me silly. Since it
doesn't, we go at it full force sweating and grunting. I'm
sucking her tiny pink nipples. Her hair is crazy in my hands.
I'm smelling the maple odor from her hairy armpit like it was
the world's rarest perfume. I'm kissing and sucking her every

which way. My tongue is begging me to say that if it could just rent some space in her asshole I could die happy. Before I know it I'm biting off the buttons of her long black schoolmarm skirt and I feel warm liquid ooze down my leg and creep into the arch of my shoe. She isn't wearing any underwear. Intent boils over. Her cunt is so intoxicating I sniff her like a junkie and nod out into her sweet gash, losing myself in her God wound that I try to fix within the confines of my mouth. I wish I had a dick to fuck her. I know I don't need one as I stick my three fingers into her pussy and groove it to her in rhythm with her moans, but I wish for one. I want to know what it would feel like having a throbbing baby arm to slide in and out of her. I tell her if I had a dick I'd fuck her, so good like no man could. I feel my crotch burning and throbbing like I'm rejecting some low-riding abortion. I pull off my pants and try to enter with what I think is my penis.

This insistent weapon, this tool of fuck, this goddamned father tongue slapping me in the stomach lightly as if to politely say, "Excuse me, ma'am," woke me from the depths of my sweet dream. I said, "Holy mother," out loud when I realized I was conscious, unable to hide. I sat up blown bewildered. It begged my hand to touch it. I was almost afraid to. It looked so foreign as it spoke in tiny throbs like a squirming flesh-and-blood lollipop. So to appease it I started out slow, grabbing at the balls. My balls. I thought of Johnny, my best bud. He would crack completely if he saw this pair of kiwis hanging off my crotch. "How?" I asked myself. "And why the fuck now?"

When in doubt, jerk off.

My hand raced mechanically. All those years of watching finally paid off. My body curved backward in pleasure in seamless time with the speed of my hand. I came in all of three minutes. And they're all right about it, all those guys: it's unexplainable. After I figured out aim, I jerked off three more times. All I could think about was the librarian. The curve of her ass. Her full mouth. Her eyes weighted with the dark intelligence of wars, suicides, plagues. I wanted her to run me down. Pull me apart. Take my body and burn it. Then, if it would please her, to smoke my remains with experienced relish. It's embarrassing to admit it, but when I did come I managed to hit my mirror, my eye, and the picture of my mom that was sitting so innocently on my dresser. It was all pretty exciting but I wasn't exactly sure if I liked the idea. My cunt hadn't disappeared (of course I checked) so I wasn't going to freak out. I resigned myself to thinking that I could always have the damned thing removed like that mole I had cut off my ass some years back.

After some spare thoughts of pissing in my dad's mouth I lay back in bed. My mind, coursing a steadier thread to oneness, concentrated on entering the wet gateway of the librarian. If the recollection felt like this, what would the real thing feel like? Why the hell did I have to wake up? Instead of sulking I made a decision. I set out to do what any man with a dick should do: please a woman righteously.

I called in sick. What? You expect me to tell the boss I got myself a dick and I don't know what to do? I didn't call anyone else, because no one would have believed me. Hell, I sure wouldn't have.

On the street I felt like laughing in the face of every passerby. I wondered vaguely if terrorists with bombs felt this way, godlike and secretive.

As I was coming out of the deli with my pack of morning smokes some cabbie asked me if I wanted a ride. I said no thanks. To push it further he told me, "Well, that's some ass you got on ya, honey." I said, "Yeah?" And he said "Yeah." So I stepped a bit closer to him. I cupped my tits lovingly and asked if he liked these as well. He was getting all excited, fidgeting in his seat and licking his lips like they were candied. "I'd give each of those pups a ten, sweetie, how's about you and me going somewhere quiet for a while?" So I start to unbutton my jeans on the street. "Hey hey hey," he was saying, all slack mouth and joke glasses. With inherent dramatic flair I whipped out my dick.

I savored the softness of his lust imperceptibly turning into shocked disgust when I asked him how he liked it and if he thought it was bigger than his. Skid marks, sister. Skid marks and smoke.

As I walked my secret began to give me away. I was forced to visit a used-book store and buy a large physics textbook to hide the hard-on that kept erupting every time I even so much as smelled a female. Cartoonish, practically on the verge of shooting lava on anyone in firing range, slowly I became deranged. My tits felt like they were deflating. Am I a man or a fucking blow-up doll? Inside nuclear vengeance slapped around my genetic code. I walked into the bar with a bristly face and a warhead pointing downward from the doorstep of my pelvis. I don't drink but decided to try anything in order to get out of the naked afternoon, which began to haunt me with its perky exuberance.

I was hoping for a bit of darkness to surround me and give me some kind of answer. Thankfully the place was empty. I would have some time to think about this thing. I didn't ask for it. Not really. Did I? I couldn't say. The age-old question pulverized.

The bartender was a fine-looking female. The place was quiet and smelled vaguely of crack cocaine and piss. It didn't matter to the dick, though. The dick thought everything was just great, especially when something fell and the bartender bent over to retrieve it. I was humiliated, but the dick didn't care. I couldn't keep my eyes off her. I felt possessed, invaded, and horrified at my own leering position. She stared blankly into the interior of her book. I could tell by her nervous body movements that I was making her uncomfortable. My own uneasiness dissolved swiftly, along with my mental capacity to see her as another human and not some tool to instant pleasure.

The phone rang and jolted me a couple of inches off my stool. She didn't seem to notice. She walked slowly over to the red ringing. Then her hand dangling that long hard plastic receiver was placed so close to her mouth it drove me insane. I watched her baited through the throat as she parted her lips. She stared into the mouthpiece in annoyed disbelief and then said a firm no into it before slamming it down.

As she walked back to her perch my eyes were glued to the crotch of her jeans. The material there seemed to be buried deep in her snatch. I imagined slick salvation. I wiped my mouth and tried instead to concentrate on a roach just disappearing into the sticky metal opening of a draft tap. Her breasts were a good size. They belonged in my mouth.

She didn't care about me. In fact I was probably bothering her just breathing. She shifted her position and asked me if I was all right. I had been meditating on being a bead of sweat caught in her ass crack. I said, "I have a dick, you know." Just like that. The thing I hadn't wanted to say coming out loudest. She kinda laughed and said, "Whatever," which pissed me off for some reason. She sensed the weather and added jokingly, "I've got one too; his name is Frankie." She laughed, proud of her own joke. She seemed to be laughing at me. I imagined her in a garden of sprouting helpless phalluses. Pulling the rip cord on a hungry lawn mower and cutting them down with that laugh; sucking them into her cunt, never to be heard from again.

I could no longer feel my clit or my slit. I think at this point I was one hundred percent dick. I asked for another. She said just like a smart-ass, "Ain't you going to finish the one you got?" I said, "It's too warm," and I was sweating but it was because of this bitch you see with the unforgiving eyes and her tight ass too good for anyone. Too good for me. She shrugged and went to grab the handle of my mug. I clocked her one across the face. She was so close to me that the force of my fist made her hit the back wall squarely. I leaped over the bar and grabbed her by her hair. "Look, all I want to do is fuck your sweet little prize." She tried to look around wildly for help so I grabbed her mane tighter. She spat in my face and that seemed to make my dick harder. I straddled her leg and pushed my hard-on against her hip and then grabbed my mug from the bar and broke the glass, holding a jagged piece up to her tender throat. I told her to shut the fuck up and if she did something like that again she'd be sorry. I was so exhilarated my chest burned with a lottery of molten superman insignias. I told her I was going to let go of her hands so I could tape her up so she shouldn't try anything funny.

She began to cry and say please and for a moment she reminded me of my librarian. I told her, "Don't worry, I'll show
you a good time. I'll make you come all over. Just don't make
me hurt you." Although to tell you the truth I wanted to fuck
her apart with my shotgun shooter. I wanted her to scream
agony as I pulsed my white weakness through her that she un-
covered so well and laughed at. Smug self-serving bitch.

I punched her hard. She fell whimpering. I grabbed a roll
of tape off the shelf and went to work. Woefully I rammed a
wad of napkins in her mouth. She had such a sweet mouth,
full and ripe like fresh bits of orange. I was sorry to see it replaced by the silver square. Bye-bye, mouth. I thought about
her sucking my cock in there. Her eyes loving me and hating
me the whole time. She'd probably bite it off if she could. I
wasn't having any of that.

I pushed her head down. I tore her shirt off from behind.
With a knife I found in the sink I cut off her bra straps and
freed her tits. She shuddered when she felt the metal touch.
The place was so quiet except for her moans and my heavy
breathing. Bits of light meandered in as if to say we were in
hell and paradise was just right outside. I bent her over at her
waist and checked out her ass. It was Eden enough for me.
She was my whore; my little sinning apple; my bitch; mine;
mine; my ass; my pussy; my fuck box; my warm twitching toy.

I picked her up by her belt and turned her over. I unbut-
toned her jeans and pulled them down past her knees. I
spread her legs apart. I rubbed her cunt before I cut off her
panties. She had a beautiful piece. Her wetness betrayed her.
Maybe it was because she had pissed her pants. Maybe it was
because she wanted me. She tried to wriggle away. I smashed

her head against the black tile. "Don't move, you impatient cunt! I'm getting to that, don't you worry." She shook her head no, but we all know what she meant to say was yes.

I unbuckle, unzip, and unleash myself and enter. In my right hand I've got her head pulled back and I'm ramming it in with everything I've got. I'm feeling her jiggling tit in my left hand and I feel just like God. She's my dog; my horse; my fucking amusement park ride. It's so damned warm in the pussy fuck shit damn it's goddamned scorching in there. Move it bitch! Move it or I'll cut you. The walls of her cunt spasmed against me like an ocean of epileptic fit. I felt like I was going to decompose, explode, dismantle. I don't want to come in her cunt. I hold myself back. I want her ass. I want to be in her ass. I want my sperm in her ass. I don't want her to forget me, boy. She ain't ever going to forget me. I enter her asshole; it's a tight velvet doorway. I spread her ass cheeks until my balls rub against her pink hairy crack. As I come I feel myself shrinking, rapidly becoming minuscule, infinitesimal.

Where am I?

Who is this girl?

What the hell am I doing?

I pull away from her. I see this pair of bodiless testicles hanging out of this girl's ass but I can't believe my own eyes. I feel like I've done something wrong, but I don't know how. I'm kneeling on broken glass. She looks hurt, afraid. I look down at my own cunt. Blood is spurting everywhere. I can't speak.

I'm running now.

Wind on my face.

Librarian?

What have I done with my sweetness?

Daily Agenda

S A R A H   B .   W E I R

1. wake up with wood
2. harass slumbering bedmate
3. leave toilet seat up
4. create copious steam and soap scum
5. shave cheeks and chin
6. consider running for office or joining clergy
7. apply Rogaine, flexing
8. hurriedly deposit bowl of sodden bran buds in sink
9. grab large coffee and a Danish to go
10. pause at construction site; meditate on heavy machinery
11. greet personal assistant, send on personal errands
12. fart noisily at arriving business partner
13. hold all calls
14. exit to john, with newspaper

15. contemplate switching careers to architecture, law, or fine-furniture making
16. compliment assistant's beautiful hair
17. flip through Sharper Image catalog
18. fantasize
19. covertly compare dick with that of nearby urinal user
20. devour two hot dogs
21. smile with genuine kindness at female pedestrians
22. arrive late for prostate screening
23. labor over timesaving computer system
24. close office door
25. plan all-male trip to forest area with guns
26. make assistant initiate calls to associates who are holding calls
27. peruse sports section
28. call bookie
29. debate with business partner over best-qualified *Sports Illustrated* swimsuit model
30. call wife
31. call friends
32. call wife to warn of late arrival
33. hug dog; greet wife
34. flip between news channels while reading Victoria's Secret catalog and other important mail
35. fetch microbrewery beer; appreciate lawn from kitchen window
36. shake hands with visiting son
37. during dinner argue in favor of castration of rapists
38. clear own plate and flatware, leave glass and napkin

39. putter
40. watch X v. Y game; lose money silently
41. shake hands with exiting son
42. scratch
43. pee off back porch
44. doubt significance of own life
45. read Introduction to *The Seven Habits of Highly Effective People*
46. fail to obtain erection
47. leave toilet seat up; ignore drips
48. toss and turn
49. fall asleep on couch
50. snore

The Pricks in Physics: A Historical Fantasy

MARGARET WERTHEIM

What a difference a dick would have made to Margaret Cavendish, the duchess of Newcastle. A woman of the seventeenth century, Cavendish yearned to be part of the scientific revolution going on around her. Yet despite the myth of objectivity, for most of its history science has been a pursuit open only to those possessing a penis. Cavendish was actually one of the lucky women of her age, with her title and wealth she was effectively able to make herself an honorary dick for a day—for one day, at least. It was a bright clear day in 1667 when she was granted the privilege of visiting a working session of the English Royal Society—one of the first, and still, perhaps, the most prestigious, of all scientific societies. Mind you, the visit had not been easy to arrange. The duchess's request had been met by the society's members with nothing short of alarm. When this august institution had been founded just a few years before, its first secretary, Henry Oldenburg, declared that its mission was "to raise a Masculine Philosophy . . . whereby the Mind of Man may be ennobled by knowledge of Solid Truths." That a woman should now seek to walk among them challenged the integrity of that manly enterprise.

The upstart duchess had indeed been doing just that, for she had already written several books on the new philosophy of nature and had disputed both Descartes's dualism and Hobbes's theory of matter. But such a woman could not be dismissed lightly. Wealthy as well as noble, Cavendish was a generous patron of Cambridge University, and her money would be most welcome to the fledgling Royal Society. The duchess's request for a visit thus threw its members into turmoil. Finally, after much debate, it was agreed that she should attend a session in which Robert Boyle would perform one of his famous experiments with the air pump. And so, on the appointed day, Cavendish was allowed to enter the inner sanctum of science as a spectator. But it was to be the *only* day on which she set foot in those hallowed halls.

Margaret Cavendish's title and wealth could buy her a day among the men of science—but no more. Without a member she could never be a Member, and remained an outsider to the official scientific community, writing and publishing her books in intellectual isolation. The bastion of British science did not fully accept a woman into its ranks until 1945, almost three centuries after it opened; as historian Londa Schiebinger has wryly noted: "For nearly three hundred years, the only permanent female presence at the Royal Society was a skeleton preserved in the society's anatomical collection." Moral of the story: in the halls of science, without a dick you'd be better off dead.

⚲

A dick would most certainly have come in handy to Mary Somerville, another Englishwoman, who sought to be part of the physics community a century and a half later. No other science has been so consistently and persistently female-free. The value of a penis to a physicist was especially evident on the day in 1832 when the Royal Society sent Somerville a letter informing her that as thanks for her contributions to physics and astronomy they had commissioned a bust of her to stand in their Great Hall. The letter declared that the male members would "honor Science, their country and themselves, in paying this proud tribute to the powers of the female mind." Yet their acknowledgment of her mind pointedly did not extend to opening their doors to its bearer. If Somerville had had a dick that day, it would not have been a marble bust, but her physical presence that would have been welcomed into the Great Hall.

For Mary Somerville, most days would have been different had she possessed a penis. While her brother received first-class schooling in preparation for the university, as a dickless daughter Mary was given only a rudimentary education—just one year at Miss Primrose's boarding school. Yet even as a girl Somerville hungered for knowledge and taught herself Latin. Later she was drawn to mathematics and, determined to pursue this mysterious subject, borrowed her brother's textbooks and began to teach herself. So alarmed were her parents by such unorthodox behavior in a young lady that they removed the candles from her room so she couldn't read at night. Somerville responded by memorizing the problems and working on them in her head. Not until she won a medal in a mathematics competition did anyone take her interest seriously.

Without formal training Somerville could not become a major force in physics; nonetheless, she made an invaluable contribution to the field. Although England had once been the undisputed leader in physics, by the early nineteenth century it had dropped well behind. During the eighteenth century the baton had passed to France, where one of the ever-so-seminal scientific achievements of the age was the monumental book by Pierre Simon Laplace on the motions of the planets and stars. Laplace's work on celestial mechanics had proved once and for all that the heavens were ruled by Newton's laws, and that no divine intervention was necessary to keep the celestial orbs gliding along their paths. But in spite of its importance, this work had not been translated into English, and so British science lagged behind.

Somerville took on the task of rectifying this omission; she spent years painstakingly translating Laplace's legendarily difficult tome. To the basic text she added copious notes, explanations, and mathematical derivations to assist the reader. Once finished, her book became a standard text for advanced students at Cambridge University. Yet while her book was taught there, as a woman she was not permitted to sit in the university's lecture halls as either a student or a teacher. Thus, on any day of the week, one could rest assured that the budding physicists poring over Somerville's text would all be the proud possessors of a penis.

✿

One day in the history of physics when a dick proved positively indispensable was the day they handed out the 1944 Nobel Prizes. On that day the German chemist Otto Hahn was awarded a Nobel for his work on nuclear fission—the process that lies at the heart of nuclear bombs and power plants. The Austrian physicist Lise Meitner, who was the official leader of Hahn's team, and who also worked out the theoretical explanation of their experimental discoveries, was not even mentioned in the Nobel committee's announcement. Many of the committee's decisions have raised eyebrows, but in this case there is wide agreement that the prize rightly belonged to Meitner as well. One cannot help but wonder: if Meitner had had a dick that day, would she have been so readily denied a share in science's greatest honor?

The value of a dick was already evident on another day in Meitner's life, when her destiny became clear to her. On that day, while just a child, Meitner noticed a puddle of water with an oil slick on top catching the light and making the puddle gleam with all the colors of the rainbow. What could be causing this shimmering magic? The answer Lise was given entranced her, and the young girl became convinced that if she worked hard enough she, too, would come to understand nature's laws. Unfortunately, Austria's laws allowed only those citizens with penises to attend the high schools that prepared students for university. Citizens without penises were expected to marry those who had them, but much to her parents' dismay, Meitner showed no interest in that goal. She wanted to be a physicist.

Eventually, her father agreed to hire her a physics tutor, but only on the condition that she first secure her employment prospects by spending three years gaining a school teaching certificate. Meitner later called these her "lost years" and believed she suffered all her professional life from the loss of that precious time. In 1901, after Austria finally opened its universities to women, she was at last able to begin her education in science.

After taking her doctorate, Meitner became fascinated by radioactivity and moved to the University of Berlin to pursue further study and research. There she teamed up with Hahn and a fruitful partnership began. There was just one problem: the institute where they set up their equipment had a rule that no persons without penises were allowed in the building. In the end a compromise was reached: Meitner could do her work out of sight in the basement, but she was not allowed upstairs in the real laboratories. Occasionally the shy Austrian broke this rule and sneaked upstairs to hide under the tiers of seats to listen to a lecture. With a dick for a day she could, of course, have sat comfortably with the other learned pricks.

Years later, after the Meitner-Hahn team had split up, the field of radioactivity was thrown wide open and Meitner found herself at the center of one of the major challenges of twentieth-century physics. The dream of the alchemists—the transmutation of one element into another—had been achieved. Atoms of uranium had been transformed into something else. The question was, What? And by what atomic process? As a world leader in radioactivity, Meitner assembled a team that once again included Hahn, and they threw themselves into the problem. Hahn led the experimental work, with constant advice from Meitner, but it was she who came up with the brilliant theoretical explanation of how a uranium atom could be broken apart into several smaller atoms. Nonetheless, when the Nobel committee announced its award Hahn alone was named.

Thirteen years later the Chinese-American particle physicist Chien-Shiung Wu would similarly be left out when the Nobel committee made its announcements. This time Wu was the chief experimenter investigating the principle known as symmetry breaking, but the prize went only to the two dick-endowed theorists who proposed the idea. Only two women have ever won the physics Nobel: Marie Curie, a woman of the nineteenth century, and Marie Goeppert Mayer, who was awarded the prize in 1963.

As late as the 1950s a physicist without a dick literally had to watch her step. In a recent autobiography, the nuclear physicist Fay Ajzenberg-Selove reported that during that decade she was invited by colleagues at Princeton's physics department to use the university's cyclotron for a series of experiments, but since the department chairman had a rule—"No women in the building"—she had to creep around at night to do her work. The Harvard physics department did not accept dickless physicists on its faculty until the 1970s, when it was forced to do so by antidiscrimination law; and as of mid-1996, Princeton's physics department has still not granted tenure to a physicist not sporting the penile appendage.

At a time when women have become presidents, astronauts, fighter pilots, Supreme Court justices, and racing car drivers, not a single woman has ever headed a particle accelerator facility, the pinnacle of the physics establishment. But perhaps this should not surprise us. After all, what are these machines if not metaphoric dicks? Take a look at one: it's a huge powerful protrusion that, once aroused, spurts jets of potent particles. Once upon a time men claimed that the secret power of life resided in their sperm; now physicists claim that the secret power of the universe is to be found in the orgasmic spurts of their accelerators. And just as the humble joe obsesses about the size of his "equipment," so, too, the particle physicist obsesses about a bigger, more powerful piece—one capable of penetrating ever deeper into Nature's secrets.

For my own part, I wish that once during my six years studying physics and mathematics I could have had a dick for a day. What would it be like not to be the anomaly? What would it be like to be just one of the boys, instead of some misfitting "other"? What would it be like not to feel I constantly had to justify my presence and not to see that hint of condescension in the eyes of physicists when I walked in the door? What would it be like not to have constantly to prove that I might—just might—actually know something about physics? In the late seventeenth century, the early feminist educator François Poullain de la Barre proclaimed the ability of women to participate in the enterprise of science and wrote that "the mind has no sex." While it is undoubtedly true that the minds of women are as able as the minds of men to study the world around us, the field of physics continues to be refracted through the eye of the penis. With a dick for a day, I, too, could have a prick's-eye view.

VICTORIA ROBERTS

IF I HAD A DICK FOR A DAY, I'D SIT AT HOME QUIETLY AND WAIT FOR IT TO GO AWAY.

Dick W. and His Pussy; or, Tess and Her Adequate Dick

JANE YOLEN

Once upon a time—I say that up front so you will know this is a fairy tale and not just another wish-fulfillment fantasy—there was a boy named Adequate Dick. Unfortunate, but true. His mother, being no better than she should have been, but a beauty nonetheless, named him after that which had brought her much fame though little fortune.

When she saw that having a child narrowed her client base, she abandoned him. Simply dropped him off at the nearest dock: Whittington Pier. If she had dropped him *off* the dock instead of *at* it, this story would have been considerably shorter.

Adequate Dick knocked about the port for quite some time, about fifteen years to be exact, eventually taking the dock's name as his own, after much pier counseling. He was handsome; in that, he took after his mother. But in all other ways he was like his dad: adequate.

At last one day he was hired by a kind merchant who was always on the lookout for cheap labor.

"Will you come and work for me, Adequate Dick Whittington Pier?" asked the merchant.

"I will," said Adequate Dick.

They shook hands but signed no papers. In those days no one could write, though most had handshakes down pat.

Now, the boy quickly came to the attention of the merchant's pretty daughter, Tess, who had a fondness for lower-class Dicks. She gave him money and considerable other favors, which Adequate Dick, being well named and handsome but not particularly favored in the brains department, took as a compliment.

He took a few other things as well: her silver ring, a glass vase, a small nude portrait done on ivory. He didn't take Tess's virtue. She had none left for him to take.

The merchant knew that cheap labor has a way of drifting, and so to keep his servants happy and at home, he gave them certain allowances. He allowed them once a year to give him something of theirs to take on his voyage, something the merchant might sell to make their fortunes. None of them ever got rich this way, of course. But, as if it were a sixteenth-century lottery, the chance of becoming millionaires overnight kept all the servants trying and at home. *Very* trying and *quite* at home.

Adequate Dick had nothing to give the merchant but a cat named Pussy (and the things he had taken from Tess, but those he would not part with). But when it was his turn, he handed over his pet without a thought. "Pussy could make my fortune," he thought, thereby proving himself his mother's boy. The vegetable does not fall very far from the tree.

Tess could have warned him that his chances for a fortune were slim at best. But she didn't want him leaving anyway. "Why waste a perfectly adequate Dick?" was her motto.

🜗

So far—I can hear you saying—this sounds like a folktale, what with the merchant and his pretty daughter, a servant and his cat. Or maybe it sounds like the plot of an eighteenth-century picaresque novel. Or a grainy, naughty black-and-white French film. But how can it be a fairy tale? It has no fairies in it. Or magic.

And you would be right. Right—but impatient.

Wait for it.

The merchant's ship ran aground on a small island kingdom and he was thought lost to the world. The household, like a boat, began to founder; the servants to look for other work. Adequate Dick, being last hired, was first fired, so he went off toward the familiar docks to seek his fortune. Without—of course—his Pussy. Either one.

So what of Tess?

She tried to take over her father's firm. She was the merchant's only child, after all. But the men who worked for her complained.

"She has," they said, "no Adequate Dick. And who can run a business without one?" It was true. Her Adequate Dick had gone back to his piers.

Then a miracle!

You must allow me a miracle.

Surely miracles will do in a tale when magic is nowhere to

be found. Miracles *are* magic processed by faith and a lack of a scientific imagination.

The merchant returned home unexpectedly, but just in time it seems, with much gold in his ship's hold. The island kingdom where he had run aground had itself been overrun by rats. That he had Pussy to sell was a great fortune. Or a miracle. Or a serendipity. Or a fairy tale. Or the kind of luck a Donald Trump would envy. (Speaking of adequate Dicks.)

So he sold Dick's Pussy. But little did he know the consequences of such a sale. For miracles are not singular. They lean on one another, like art on art. No sooner was Pussy sold than Tess—far away in London—found herself changed beyond measure. That is, she could measure the change. It occurred between her legs.

Was she surprised? Not really. It was merely form following function.

The merchant returned home rich beyond counting.

"Where is that Adequate Dick?" he asked when he entered the door.

"Oh, Father!" Tess cried. "He has gone. But something rare has occurred. Something better than Adequate."

Her father did not listen. He was not a man to believe in the miraculous beyond the swelling of a purse. "Better get him back, then," he said. "He has wealth and treasure."

"As do I," thought Tess, pausing to spit accurately by the stoop. Then she ran down the road to call Adequate Dick home, crying: "Turn again, Whittington Pier." She had never called him by his first name outside her bedroom.

He heard her, and he turned.

And returned.

Now that he was rich, Tess could marry him, though, given the circumstances, she never slept with him again. He was no longer of the lower classes and he was—after all— only an *adequate* Dick.

She had better.

MARISA ACOCELLA

If I had a penis and I was having sex with a woman I would just make her come so many times, to make up for all the times I didn't. I don't think my personality would change, as I pretty much do what I want. I guess I'd like to use my penis as a tool for women's pleasure—and probably jerk off in the shower, because I wouldn't want to get my sheets dirty.

Café Star (Coming Soon Near You)

JENNIFER BLOWDRYER

If I were a white man, more people would like me. Attacks from women and minorities would not be frontal; they would come in the form of behind-the-scenes grumbling. Would I be a nice white man? Probably not.

Hell no, I would not be a nice white man. Right now, with my scars, internal wounds, and lack of exercise, at the age of thirty-four, I am mildly good-looking. As a man I, like the father I resemble, would be gorgeous. Scars are sexy, only really fat men get cellulite, wounds are the stuff of brooding intrigue. Sex with women would not even be my endgame, as sex with men is now.

Fadingly pretty women, the kind I'm surrounded by, would take in their breath a little when I was around, fawn over my tiny statements, but I'd never fuck them, these second-class citizens of the interesting outfit.

I'd marry a beautiful artist, and fuck the prize girls if I

could. Some young thin girl, I'd sweet-talk. She'd be sitting there, slim, pretty, and trashed, at my bar gig. It would be romantic, this small show, reading my poetry, doing an approximation of some other singer, the way I was starting to lose my looks just a little.

I am a grizzled romantic at this bar, both a wounded little boy and a sexy scarred drink-ticket warrior, too independent, too free, from the mediocre compromise of society. Of course, being white, I presumably had an option, somewhere around late junior high. This shabbiness is a primal choice, not a case of poor planning on my part.

This skinny girl would wait for me, flush during my set, her whole body knowing I was there. I can wait to get around to her; there is the amplifier to see to, the serious matters of my bass player and stipend. Finally, in my own good time, I'm ready to leave the bar. She is there, plastered to my aura but a couple of respectful feet away, so there that I don't even need to say, "C'mon." I don't even have to say, as Mick Jagger once crooned, "No, I don't want to see your ID—I can see that you're so far from home!"

She's got some name, she's some Sherry or Marissa or Susie, this girl, we all have these generic names now, women and men. Mike, Tom, Kevin, Jennifer, what have you, names hardly matter.

When I say this as a woman I'm a shrill eccentric, when I say this as a man, a man called, say, Mark, it is gruff, part of the little edge of bewilderment I hide beneath the stubble.

We're walking to my apartment now; I'm wheeling my fucking equipment along, as usual. Marissa is starting to talk now, breathlessly, careful not to say anything. My identity is the compelling one around here, after all. She's talking about how she couldn't get her first beer, how good I am, how they just don't get it, the magnitude of my rusty little spin in the limelight. *Clack, clack, clack,* her heels are scuttering along, the sound holding just about as much meaning as her prattle, *clack clack clack.*

Yes, this Susan or what have you is thrilled, she has made it inside the door of my place. There is some disarray here, but not woman-falling-apart debris, this is important-guy-with-no-time-for-frills clutter. What I have to do is the next thing. "When I was a boy," crooned the Beatles, "everything was ri-hight." Well, something was right, usually me. Some time between the ages of fourteen and eighteen I slugged my stepfather, whipped his ass good, and this proves it. The holidays are not an Issue, they are a bunch of days. I'll get something nice for my kid, the one in New Jersey or Florida.

After I put down my equipment, there is the issue of Jeanine, whoever, to turn to. You'd almost forgotten about her too, hadn't you? She seems all right. Anyway, "Hey," and here she is. I look at her body, thinking I am alone in this glance. Actually, women always notice. They pretend they don't for the sake of mystery, or is it tact. Words, these are just words, almost but not quite as important as, say, cigarettes. Does she have one? Ah, well.

She'll begin our night at home, some more pretty talk, talk like charms. All I have to do is follow the surface, of where she's from or who did what; beneath this is her sweet little body, the cuteness of her deceptions, the beautiful ignorance of her admiration, her body. Slowly I reach for her. You have to wait these women out a little; patience is part of being the lover they'll want again. Their halter tops and flat pierced bellies don't mean, but then again they do.

The prattle is winding down. She's satisfied with her little dialogue, the anxiety puttering away with each statement, each excuse; women live in these little glances, not in their endless ridiculous analysis, their inanely inclusive plans. You've got to know this, move slowly.

But not too slowly. Too slow makes you as much of a whimpering idiot as them, the last thing they want. They don't fuck their girlfriends, for the most part, do they? Grab something hard, an arm, the body, a hand, take over now. Relieve them of their own trivia, this absurd worriedness. Take something off her after a minute. Her body inspires; take the girl. Love her, it's not hard, her lies are sweet, ancient, her lies are an apron, a plate of Christmas cookies, careful wrapping paper.

This girl, this woman, has been part of the night. If I'm lonely I need her; if I'm not, I don't. This Janet will writhe in tension for days afterward, checking her phone machine every five minutes, maneuvering casual encounters, calling with nothing to say.

Whatever; I've got stuff to do. With any luck, this night with Keiko won't matter. It sure as hell wasn't about good and evil, that release into a new body.

Where did I *just* put my pack?

Flower Girl Pinup

AVA GERBER

Penis Parlor

LISA HILL

Leigh looked at the clock behind the lectern. Only five more minutes to go. She decided to wind the lecture up early. "In other words, do women really speak in a 'different moral voice,' as Gilligan claims, or do you agree with her critics that the 'different' voice she hears is merely the 'higher voice' of patriarchy? You decide; only I'd like your answers in my mailbox by five o'clock today."

Back in her office, Leigh looked out the window and down at the streams of students dawdling off to class. She watched a plane slowly make its way along the horizon to somewhere else, and took the next paper from her stack. Student No. 954499393. Kim Gordon. "Men and women are different; they are very very different in many ways physically, mentally, and emotionally, and hell, women are smarter!"

Leigh groaned and threw the paper back on the stack. It was beginning to dawn on her that her lectures were being delivered to students with hermetically sealed brains. Down in the quadrangle, somebody's dog sniffed at strewn sandwich wrappers and empty Coke cans. The frayed piece of rope attached to its collar dragged on the ground as it sniffed and wandered aimlessly, passing the time while it waited to be reclaimed. Leigh watched for a while before launching a second assault on the offending paper. This time, she managed to make it to the end. *Lower pass.* "Kimberly, Some interesting thoughts here; however, there is little evidence of research. Sweeping claims based on 'personal experiences with my boyfriend' do not constitute social science, at least not in this department. Political science is a discipline, not a mood. The relevance of certain claims (e.g., your endorsement of Freud's theory of penis envy in women) was not made sufficiently clear. By the way, 'gender' is not spelled with a 'j.' "

It was time for lunch.

She walked down two flights of stairs to the English department. The walls of its corridors were hung with portraits of nineteenth-century women novelists. Why did they all look like incompetently made-up drag queens? She knocked on her friend's door. The plate on the door read "Dr. Anita Hauptmann," a moniker hard to pair with someone whose sense of humor rarely went beyond bottom jokes. She entered to find Anita hunched over her computer.

"And what is going on here, may I ask?"

"Oh, just a lot of regurgitated crap from my thesis that I'm cobbling together for a conference on postcolonialism."

Leigh remembered asking Anita once what "postcolonialism" meant, but she hadn't bothered to listen to the answer and was too embarrassed to ask again. "Let's go to lunch," she said. "I have something really weird—sick yet good—to tell you."

"Good one," said Anita as Screen Save started doing its demented thing.

🕆

They sat down at one of the cafeteria tables as an apathetic student-waiter deposited in front of them a meal they hadn't ordered. Anita leaned forward conspiratorially. "Come on, then—spill your guts."

Leigh swallowed the last of her carrot juice and scraped her hair behind her ears. Anita thought they looked like two perfect pink shells. Leigh shifted in her seat, deliberately extending the significant pause for extra effect. "I've had the op," she announced at last.

Anita pulled a disbelieving face. "You mean *the* op?" She was obviously impressed. It was normally impossible to galvanize her into anything beyond a stifled yawn.

"Yep. Extra love-tackle. And it feels fucking *fan*-tastic."

Anita's eyes gleamed as she cast them toward Leigh's lap. "Give us a look."

Leigh didn't miss a beat as she surreptitiously opened her fly under the table and eased the unimpressive-looking lump of flesh out of the gap.

Anita screwed up her nose. "It's not a stubby, is it?"

"Yeah, I know it looks a bit pathetic, but it's one of these jobs that pumps up quite well. About nine inches. I measured it."

"Not bad," Anita conceded. "Bloody ugly, though, isn't it?"

"Oh, I know. It's disgusting. They didn't have any circumcised ones left. I don't know how men have the nerve to bring them out in public. But I'm heading off to the Penis Parlor this afternoon to get it seen to."

"Oh yeah." Anita feigned indifference. "Shall I come with you? I'm writing an article on hermaphrodites as postmodern metaphor for *Ms.* magazine. It'd be great research for me."

Leigh glanced at her crotch ambivalently and hesitated. "Let me decide while I take a pee. Back in a sec."

She returned in shorter time than usual but with a peculiar, pained expression on her face.

"What's wrong with you?" Anita asked.

Leigh winced and squirmed in her jeans. "Caught the bloody thing in my zipper."

"Did it hurt?"

"Unbelievably. Bled a bit, too. I'm not used to it yet. Got a Band-Aid?"

Anita stared at Leigh's crotch and pulled a disgusted face. "Jesus, you look like you've wet yourself."

Leigh looked down and scrutinized a wet patch the size of a small apricot. "Oooh yuk. I forgot to tap. I just can't get the hang of this thing. Do you wipe it with toilet paper or what?"

Anita grimaced in revulsion. "No. I think the tap thing is right. So, can I come to the Penis Parlor with you, or what?"

"Yeah, okay," said Leigh. "But you can't watch while I get all the doo-dads done to it."

Anita remembered her own painful visits to the beautician for bikini waxes. This was likely to be worse, and watching would probably be stomach-turning. Even so, she was dying to know what it took to tart up a horrible-looking knob.

🜨

There was plenty of parking outside the Penis Parlor. Tuesday was obviously a slow day. A gaudy sign in pink neon announced that the Penis Parlor was open from ten in the morning to seven at night. The entrance was adorned with an enormous set of plastic, sugar-pink portals above which glowed a three-dimensional image of a woman standing legs apart, proudly sporting the glistening and perfectly formed accoutrements of both sexes. The evenly tanned penis of this oversized paragon of epicenism was completely hairless and devoid of any nasty-looking veins or blemishes. It looked like all the imagined penises of innocent adolescence.

They ventured into the softly lit foyer, heels sinking into thick, pink carpet. A perfectly groomed receptionist in full makeup and a helmet of stiff honey-blond hair smiled and handed them each a towel. Leigh remembered the days when every air hostess looked just like that. They turned to the menu of services on the wall and edged close to decipher the small mauve-and-gold letters:

The Penis Parlor: Beauty Is Our Duty. Double Tackle, Double Duty.
Bi-Tackle Special: Full leg, bikini line, and shaft strip: $38
Shaft and Base Strip: Only $15
Uni-Tackle Special Today only: half leg and bikini wax: $30

"Jesus, this is really weird," hissed Anita behind her hand, as they continued reading.

Why not have the works? Our Full Shaft Special, priced at $49.50, includes massage, mud pack, deodorization, and makeover. Free foundation sample to take home. Have your makeup expertly applied by a trained Shaft Beautician who will match your skin tones perfectly. Leanne was trained personally by Madame Bouvier at the Enchanté Shafte Institute in Paris, France. She brings with her a wealth of expertise and the latest techniques in "dual-apparatus" management and enhancement.

Penis Parlor uses Enchanté Shafte Beauty products exclusively.

Tanning salon open from four P.M. onward; $20 for a half-hour session.

Dr. Kanning is available for minor adjustment and enhancement surgery Wednesdays and Fridays. Please make your appointment at least a week in advance with Lois at the reception desk.

SPECIAL NOTICE: *The management regrets that Tina is away for two weeks. As a result, Penis Parlor is temporarily unable to offer its normal shaft-piercing service. Nevertheless, we would like to announce that the new summer range of rings and studs has just arrived. There is a large range of precious and semiprecious studs for your selection. We have also just taken shipment of an imported summer line of posing pouches, shaft scrunchies, and booster rings.*

All available at the accessories shop.

Leigh and Anita looked at each other furtively. Anita started giggling. Leigh punched her on the arm and announced that she'd decided to have the Full Shaft Special. She had no intention of trying out her new dong in its present condition. She'd never be able to enjoy herself worrying the whole time about how it looked and whether it smelled bad.

It didn't occur to her that she'd never once been repelled by the sight or smell of dongs wielded by *men* in her presence.

Leigh walked up to the expectant-looking receptionist. An attractive woman in a bathrobe and four-inch stilettos strolled by, her hips swaying. She paused at the door of the tanning salon to repatriate an escaped wisp of hair into an enormous arrangement of blond curls piled high on her head. As she tottered on her way, Leigh noticed the bulge jiggling at her crotch. She started to feel a little less weird.

⚘

Leigh lay on the couch and tried to relax while the beautician busied herself with heating up the wax and laying out the strips of cotton. She wore a badge bearing the Enchanté insignia; attached to it was a name tag that identified her as Michelle. Leigh wondered where the famous Leanne was today. The slight bulge at Michelle's crotch looked incongruous jutting out of the crisp, white, nurselike uniform.

Leigh ventured an inquiry. "Is this going to hurt much?"

"Have you ever had a bikini wax before?"

Leigh nodded.

"Well, this is a slightly more sensitive area, so it will hurt a bit."

How did the phrase "This will hurt a bit" translate from beautician-speak? Was it comparable to its usage in doctor-speak? Leigh hoped not. She glanced nervously in the general direction of Michelle's crotch. "Have you ever had yours waxed?"

Michelle started smearing on warm wax with a spatula. "Oh, hundreds of times. It's horrible."

"Really?" Leigh didn't much appreciate the brutal honesty of Michelle's bedside manner.

"Oh yeah. These things are a bloody nuisance, but what can you do?"

"Don't you like having it?"

Michelle pulled a face. "My shaft, you mean? Um. Oh. It's okay I suppose. Could you close your legs a little tighter please?"

She started pressing torn strips of cotton fabric onto the viscous wax. Leigh was really curious now. "But isn't it a lot of fun?"

"Geez, well . . . that's a bit of a hard one. Let me think." A short silence. "Well, I shouldn't really say this," said Michelle, lowering her voice, "because Leanne doesn't like us talking to clients about our own privates, but, quite honestly, I find mine—and I'm only speaking for myself, not generalizing or anything—but sometimes it really gets on my nerves. They do get in the way, and not having grown up with it, I still knock mine around some. I always seem to have a Band-Aid somewhere on it." Flashback to the regrettable fly incident. "Also, they can be a bit uncomfortable, especially in humid weather. All that equipment crowded into one pair of knickers can get pretty hot and sweaty down there. Not very healthy." She braced herself against the bench and prepared to rip. "Don't wear anything except cotton, if you want my advice."

Leigh tried to nod appreciatively as Michelle ripped an acre of long, coarse hairs from her groin. "Also, it used to rub against my clit constantly, so I had to start wearing a shaft support all the time, even in bed."

"Didn't that drive you insane?" Leigh gasped as she tried

to recover from the shock of the intense pain that rippled up her cock.

"Oh, yeah, it was terrible. I didn't realize how sensitive my clit was until I had something to compare it with. My boyfriend likes it, but."

"Really?"

"Yeah, it's quite ironical, because, like, he's so blokey and everything. Rugby player. Pig shooting an' all that. But he just loves it. Went mental when I wanted to have the Reverse done. He said that he pacifically forbid me from having it." She sniggered, presumably at his absurd pretensions to mastery over her.

Leigh knitted her eyebrows. "So, don't you get *any* fun out of it?" She imbued her query with as much innuendo as she could muster in her compromised condition.

"Um. A bit. Oh! I did have one really good orgasm. That was the first one. But usually it's just . . . okay. I guess I thought that because guys are—you know—horny all the time, I'd be able to get really good orgasms out of it. Lots of them. But it didn't work out like that. I prefer doing it normal, actually." She patted another cotton strip down securely and ripped it away with brutal swiftness.

Leigh gasped, suppressing a howl that badly wanted to escape from her lungs. Her eyes were watering and her dick felt as if it were being skinned alive. She gripped the sides of the bench and struggled to catch her breath in order to speak: "Yeah, I found the same thing. I've only pulled myself off once, though. Maybe it takes practice."

Michelle shrugged philosophically. "Maybe. Also, for some reason, I thought I would fuck every good-looking woman I could, but it didn't turn out that way, either."

Leigh blushed. She'd entertained the same fantasy. "What happened?"

"Oh. Um, well, I s'pose I thought my new dong would turn me into a bloke or a lezzo or whatever, but I was basically the same as before. I did try to have sex with a woman. It was really embarrassing."

"Why?"

"Couldn't get it up. Didn't fancy it I s'pose. I must be straight, eh?"

Assuming the question was rhetorical, Leigh continued with her cross-examination. "So why don't you get the Reverse done?"

"Well, I'd like to. Like, most of my friends had them off long ago. We all got ours done around the same time. My best friend, Kylie, only had hers for four days. But I can't get a Reverse—it's a condition of my continued employment here."

"Really? Is that legal? Couldn't you work somewhere else?"

"Not really." Michelle ripped off another strip of waxy cotton as Leigh strained to concentrate through the pain. "I'm only trained in Shaft Aesthetics. And I'm still under contract to Enchanté. They trained me and they also own the clinic."

Michelle was finishing now, deftly plucking the few delinquent hairs that remained on Leigh's virtually hairless pudenda. "Are you having the mud pack and the makeover as well?"

"Sure."

"I'll just rub a little aloe vera on you first, to soothe the stinging."

Leigh's flesh tingled as the cool cream was rubbed in. It felt pleasant. She started to feel a lot better as Michelle applied the mud in thick, generous lashings.

Leigh was left alone with her thoughts for fifteen minutes. The mud felt wonderfully healing at first, but as it dried and hardened it became unbearably itchy. Michelle returned, removed the mud, and produced a large card that looked a bit like a paint chart. She held it against Leigh's penis, comparing the various tints with Leigh's own flesh tones. She looked at Leigh directly for the first time. "So why did *you* get one?"

Leigh wondered paranoically if people could tell she was an academic. Did she look too bookish to be carnal? Yet she was starting to ask herself the same question. She tried to think of an answer, and a number of possibilities sprang to mind: she'd been curious; she'd fantasized about the insights it would bring to her work on gender politics; everyone was doing it; it seemed like a cool thing to do. But "Buggered if I know" was the answer she gave.

She was amazed at her own words. For someone who normally analyzed the living shit out of everything, it sounded pretty lame. A silence fell between them. Michelle started experimenting with tints. She dabbed a little color on. "Um, still a few too many orange undertones in there. What season are you?"

"Spring, I think."

"Yeah. I think you're right, but you've also got a tiny bit of winter in there as well."

"Probably. I have a lot of trouble getting the right shade of lipstick." The browns were always too brown; the reds too pink. Leigh was more interested in pursuing her organ inquiries. "So, exactly how painful is the reverse op?" She'd been so excited at the prospect of enjoying her new penis, she hadn't even considered the alternative.

"Oh, it's a hell of a lot simpler than the attachment. A few nips and tucks. Only takes about twenty minutes under a local."

Leigh lay back and contemplated the mauve ceiling tiles again. She closed her eyes as Michelle hummed softly to herself, blending, smoothing, and shading. "I'll just give the tip and base a hint of blusher, and you can tell me what you think." She held the mirror to Leigh's immaculately primped member. Even as she beheld the pinkness and neatness of her rehabilitated cock, Leigh felt uneasy.

🎎

She found Anita awaiting her return in the foyer and reading a magazine called *Bi-Tackle Monthly*. On the cover was a photograph of a pretty, dark-haired woman posing in a specially designed bathing suit. There were seams and ruches at the crotch, which accommodated and accentuated the owner's extensions. The happy, unself-conscious look on the model's face, the gentle tilting of her crotch toward the camera, made Leigh feel slightly squeamish.

Anita put the magazine down and smiled expectantly. "So? How was it? What have you got for me?"

Leigh looked at her blandly. "Nothing really. Though I do have one thing to say."

"And what, pray tell, is that?"

Leigh smiled. "Sigmund Freud was a thorough twit."

META MORPHENIX

verse Barbara O'Dair　　graphics Hannah Alderfer/Marybeth Nelson　　story Rachael Carron

CONTENTS OF PURSE:
10:17 AM
mirror
tissues
datebook
change purse
lipstick
handful of condoms

CONTENTS OF PURSE:
7:33 PM
handful of condoms
tube of KY jelly
a cock ring
a wad of
toilet paper
pamphlet for
a do it yourself
prostate exam
a sock

CONTENTS OF PURSE:
3:04 AM
a sock
a pencil
a banana
a cucumber
a cigar
a postcard of the
Empire State Building

I could try to tell you this in a straightforward way.

I could exercise a little detachment, treat it as a lab or police report, at least as some mildly sensationalist piece of journalism. Somehow it doesn't seem appropriate.

One has ways of knowing things, of realizing facts very efficiently. Our emotions are the ones that limp behind at such a pathetic pace. Our evolution has been somewhat lopsided, all that innovation that has us lording it over the planet doesn't seem to have extended to the softer places: the heart and that part of the head that governs our less rational features.

And so, it was a surprisingly brief encounter that persuaded me of the fact that on a Tuesday morning in January I woke up with a penis. (I am omitting to add that I have been a woman my whole life; it's the sort of thing I presume you would have known, but I am learning not to presume). When I woke up that morning there was an additional comfort to that usually provided by bed on a cold day, something more than the pocket of warmth trapped in sheets and blankets. There was a dim glowing somewhere below my middle that seemed to be conducting an entirely independent survey of the sheet folds. I have always thought that the way we check our bodies is one of the endearing reminders of our place in the animal kingdom: the way we sniff our arm pits, check our skin, pick at bits, admire our waste products, grin at our own

7. HAVE A PISS...

6. (write name in snow) SPRAY IT

5. Whip it

4. Fondle it

3. Bottle it

2. Swing it

1. "SHAKE" IT

loop-de-loop

teeth after brushing; it is more than vanity. I lifted the sheets to look at what was providing such a sense of vitality in my solar plexus, I looked because nothing very vital had been occurring there since both my estrogen levels and my husband had disappeared.

It was one of those things that at first glance you know to be just what you feared: the worst. The lump in the breast that you feel and immediately stop palpating because you are not ready for confirmation; the odd skin discoloration you roll your sleeve down to hide; the bank statement that you lose; the lover you would rather credit with deafness than disinterest. It was a penis. Not in and of itself the worst thing, but then context is everything. A fifty-five year old woman could be excused for feeling a lack of gratitude for such a development. I myself never had anything against the penis as an item. Nor did I want one for myself however. I had skipped penis envy.

It was lying in my lap, semi-tumescent, curling at an angle across my left leg. My discovery had comic potential, I have to admit, had there been an audience—comical for them. Woman lifts sheets, expression of horror crosses her recently middle-aged face, she drops sheets. I have always been able to sleep. I have slept through depression, pregnancy, illness, unemployment, a disappearing husband, just as I slept through the unwelcome realization that I had sprouted a penis. I strove to treat it as an irritant, something on the level of a lost filling.

I went back to sleep on that Tuesday morning after my brief brush with the suddenly chameleon-like behavior of my normally cooperative genitalia. I did sleep, and slept deeply without any of the large contoured dreams that you feel sure are mined somewhere deep in the storehouse of universal truths. No, just endless

23. **Walk it like a dog** 24. loop-de-loop

appearances from the supporting cast of anxiety players: dreams of broken shoe laces, holes in grocery bags, leaking ceilings, overflowing baths and one particularly undignified episode where I was wrestling with a larger than life-sized pair of men's briefs which had wrapped themselves around my middle in the canned food aisle of my local supermarket. What concerned me most in the dream was that I would be suspected of enacting an elaborate ruse enabling me to shoplift, the attack of the giant underpants did not seem to be the prime matter of concern. Perhaps this was the dream that whispered, in spite of its low buffoonery, a truth closest to what my new found form would reveal to me.

The penis was not the central problem; what harm could a penis do given the circumstances? It's not the meat, to paraphrase, it's the notion that causes the problems.

I finally emerged from bed at five o'clock. Twilight and the end of the working day, even if I was not one of those working it always provided me with a sense of relief. The struggle with the effort to be productive can be lost again as the world clocks out. On that Tuesday in January it all seemed less tragic and confusing as the cocktail hour approached. I had made some brief forays to empty my bladder during my day of sleep but had avoided any negotiation with the offending organ by stubbornly sitting and inappropriately wiping front to back rather than standing and shaking. I admire this approach in myself when I look back on those first days of what I have come to call "penishood". My defiance served me very well, it even managed to stir something resembling a silent chuckle.

15. BREAK... EACH OF THE 7 DEADLY SINS TO it ...OME COMMANDMENTS...

Butter it 16. ...DIP iT 17. 18. Plush it 19. Pluck it 20. Stuff it

Then I washed it, this new thing, showered with it. Opening the door of the shower and stepping in brought a welcome feeling of confinement, our examination room for conscience and for flesh; Pontius Pilate needed the use of a shower. To catalog and launder oneself simultaneously is such sweet penance. Alone with my new transplant in the watery confessional I can't help but blush at my own pride. There is consolation in the perfect affliction. I had been cheated of testicles. No gonads, but on this thumb of a huge man there is skin so perfectly smooth that I wonder at its composition. A new composite, skin and mercury. And it retains this liquid softness on its surface even as it grows denser, larger and more insistent.

Terminology began to preoccupy me: woman with a penis, hermaphrodite, eunuch with breasts. The word freak also floated itself into this sequence but I banished it as my washing became less rudimentary, more exploratory. This addition, this subtraction ("you haven't lost a vagina, you've

gained a penis," some fool reiterated in the tiresome speech portion of my brain) had sealed itself around my labia; a seamless job. A tender poke revealed that I hadn't actually lost my vagina. It was there behind its new addition, sheltering like a space behind a waterfall.

A man walked down the street and felt between his legs-
nothing.

A man walked down the street and felt between his legs-
twinge.

A man walked down the street and felt between his legs-
movement.

A man walked down the street and felt between his legs-
blossom.

A man walked down the street and felt between his legs-
bouquet.

A man walked down the street and felt between his legs-
1-800-FLOWERS.

A man walked down the street and felt between his legs-
delivery.

A man walked down the street and felt between his legs-
a faint memory of foliage.

My voyage of discovery was not limited to topography. Exploration leads to practical concerns. What could my new continent do for me? What surprised me was my lack of surprise, the abandoned familiarity that I brought to bear on something I might have treated with a little more diffidence, even horror. Evidence suggested that I had been fitted with the penis of a young and enthusiastic man. This is how I would think of it, consoling myself as the thought of my new state drifted in and out, trying to transform itself and always presenting the same face. I could also think of it as a version of the child's notion of creation: the conveyer belt of genitalia had randomly assigned me this particularly youthful model in an untimely administrative blunder. If desire had become for me an erratic tidal pattern this sudden imposition reversed all this and there I was with the proverbial "mind of its own." It worked.

It liked soap and water with the pressure of a tightened fist reassuring it of its new presence and swelling. I was carried away with scale. I wanted this new proportion to last, this growth of my new growth. Had my collection of travel-sized cosmetics, Russian dolls and airline liquor bottles all been a prelude to this. The appeal of the miniature and the enlargement was becoming less mysterious. This capacity for varying proportions was winning me over; I could tolerate a circus of scale. Grow to love it even. Here it was, pleasure, growing out of me with nerve endings strung out over new flesh, an architecture of points extending like an inexorable path exploding always just a little out of my reach. And then I caught up with the white spots of light r u n n i n g down its center, gathering in its tip like a chaos of revolving satellites. It was mine now; I had reached its destination.

I am the five thousand year old body frozen in an Alpine glacier and stumbled upon by diligent hikers. I am the chip of evolution suspended in ice, bar coding difference and similarity, sacrificed for use as an icon in the future. Spotted hovering in milky ice I begin a new life; my second life, life after life. A strange consolation for my premature and gruesome end. I am the prize of history to be examined, admired, expounded upon, displayed. This new second life, like the first one, not chosen, but welcome in the way of all compromises: botched reincarnation better than icy oblivion. In the end, I am glad for no choice in the matter, charmed by our resilience across the persistence of fate; armed for survival between misgivings.

I haven't tried love. Not yet. But I have seen the possibility of it drifting in, the flotsam and jetsam heralding a land mass

on the horizon. It was in a kitchen supply store, all glossy with stainless steel and copper. There were sieves and trivets, spatulas and a pot hanging on her hands and she was small, a dwarf. It was her tenacity that caught my eye. The way she negotiated all the obstacles with such defiance so that she seemed to be the essence of purpose as she reached for a pie tin on a shelf over her head or maneuvered around coagulations of shoppers bearing her load with apparent ease. I stood in line behind her waiting to pay for a lemon zester that I didn't want, standing back a little in order to look at the top of her head. I wondered about the fact that my new tube of flesh seemed to be breathing, taking in increasingly deep drafts of breath causing it to fidget and swell along a stubborn path of progress it had delineated for itself. I briefly tried to assign blame to my new organ for all of this sudden interest, but there was more. My heart was keeping time with the palpitations between my thighs and my head was not excluded from the symphony. There was an insistent curiosity growing up in my mind, as willful as the peregrinations occurring in my pelvis, what I wanted, burned to know, was how she managed to cook in a kitchen of regular dimensions, if indeed she did.

1. Encounter
Not like human and other.
Nor like human and animal.
We were scented with surprise,
seeking prey, proof or
truce, close to god, to true
oblivion.

2. Exposure
Dangling trinkets,
 secret hair,
  phantom tumors,
   butt-naked in the doorway.
    The blind self that others see
     hides from your own scrutiny.

3. Nerve
In the watery confessional,
 before the freeze,
  when all is fluid again,
   before the drowning-
You oughta hear my
long snake moan

4. Forgetting
The hinge of your mind is loosed.
A hand flips the clasp and
 grips down on the rim.
A body hoists itself out and
 scampers down the long road.

I watched her pick up a leaflet on cooking classes after she handed over her credit card. I looked after her as she raised up her shopping bags, arms lifted at right angles to prevent her shopping bags from dragging along the ground. I stared as she headed for the door utilizing the public's embarrassed deference to the different to clear a path and picking up speed as she rounded the door held open for her by incoming traffic.

On Tuesday nights I am learning the subtleties of pastry making. I look forward to these classes with more enthusiasm than I have felt in years. I wake up early on Tuesdays with a gentle fizzing in the lining of my stomach. I have even mastered choux pastry. But she is the star of the class.

Those hands that appear so blocky make pastry that tastes like it has been infiltrated by the sweetest of sea airs. I take such delight in her success that she has taken me for an ally. We eat dinner together afterwards and she orders for both of us with authority and speed. She displays such a familiarity with each of the ethnic foods she has us try that it convinces me of their desirability; I have been eating bravely. There has been no invitation to view her kitchen yet, but I am sure that it is coming. I feel she understands the timing of such invitations, just as she understands the chemistry of pastry and the lexicon of far-flung cuisine. In class next week we attempt phyllo pillows.

I would find the most beautiful woman I could and see what oral sex is like. It seems to be the one thing that all men are crazy about, so I'd really like to know if it's everything it's cracked up to be.

My Private Eye

J A N Y C E S T E F A N - C O L E

At first I ignored the big vanilla-colored envelope that arrived with the rest of my mail: bills, credit card offers, lingerie
catalogs, and pleas for lost causes—junk, I thought. Later
I was struck by the discreet gold lettering on the left-hand
corner of the wrapper: EVERYTHING YOU HAVE EVER
WANTED IS INSIDE THIS ENVELOPE. I opened it, prepared
for a blur of information, but found, instead, a simple
phrase, "You have been chosen." It sounded quasi-religious,
"chosen." I read on, thinking these ad guys had earned their
pay. I was hooked:

> If you choose, sign below and you will possess a penis for one
> day (from midnight to midnight). This is not a trick or gim-
> mick; there are no strings attached. After twenty-four hours
> your participation ends, and you will return to your female
> gender. Thank you for responding to this unique offer.

Of course, this had to be a joke. It was good, though—better than a chain letter. I saw now that there was no return address, and that the postmark was illegible. Which of my friends had cooked up this scheme? I wondered. A male for a day! I laughed as I tossed the offer back on the table.

The following evening I quarreled with my boyfriend, Barry. I asked myself why I put up with him, but it was obvious: even first thing in the morning I could look at him and say to myself, "Ooh." And in bed Barry knew me like nobody else. But when I slammed the door in his face and told him to go away, I believed I meant it this time. I was so furious I didn't know what to do. As I paced nervously around the dining table I thought, "If I was a man I'd show him!" That was when my eyes fell again on the penis-for-a-day offer. I said aloud, "Don't I wish," and hurriedly scratched my signature on the dotted line.

Strange to say, I felt better. "Good," I said, pouring myself a scotch. I sat in front of the TV and vacantly flipped stations. My cat, Enigma, slinked onto my lap, her purr motor on high. She despised Barry. I petted her neck and told her she was right, my mysterious little striped pussy.

I held my ground against Barry next morning, miserable though I was. Work was demanding all day at the office, and my schedule that night was full so I didn't have time to feel sorry for myself until I turned out the light to sleep. A pillow nursed my broken heart.

My deep slumber was disrupted before six A.M. by the phone. As soon as I heard it ring I realized I had a piercing headache. "Hello?" I said, groggily.

"Baby? Is that you? I couldn't sleep all night, talk to me."

It was him! But instead of being elated, I felt dizzy and my head was pounding. "Barry?" I said through the pain.

"Who is this?" he growled. "Put Myrna on, I want to talk to her!"

"It's me, Barry," I said, but even I noticed how deep my voice sounded. As I cleared my throat, to try to sound more like myself, my hand moved down my nightgown in a familiar gesture, toward the reassuring mound. "Oh my God!" I shouted.

"Myrna!" yelled Barry. "What's wrong? Who's there? Is he hurting you? I'll kill him! Talk to me, Myrna!"

"Barry," I said quickly, with my natural ability to cover up, "I have a sore throat. I'll call you later—we'll talk. 'Bye."

I closed my eyes and lay perfectly still. Was this really happening? I threw the covers back and looked: the sheer size of the thing frightened me, all pink and sprouting. Despite my fear, a flood of sexual imagery sent my spinning brain into a frenzy: a thigh, a nipple, lips, urges urges urges. I felt it again; it was hard now and pulsing, sticking straight up, and I was aware of a sense of weight tugging from within, creating pressure. "A cold shower!" I thought.

But I didn't want to crush my first male achievement in a cold cruel bath. Why should I? I stroked it instead, gently at first. The image of my best friend, Veronica, popped into mind—but not the Veronica I knew; this was a sexy, slutty Veronica, and I wanted to suck her completely. "Oh no," I moaned, as I rub-rubbed my new fixture until I thrust into my own hand, and . . . it was all over. I lay back, exhausted. My head stopped pounding. I was no longer dizzy. I felt relieved, but how would I ever face Veronica again? Enigma trotted into the bedroom with a warm meow. She jumped onto the bed, took one look at my naked torso, hissed, and ran away. I was a man.

I went to the toilet to piss standing up, without bothering to put the seat back down. Which reminded me of my job. I called in with the flu. My deep voice easily convinced the boss, and he told me to stay in bed; if he only knew. Mixed in with my panties I found a pair of Barry's shorts; I pulled them on and practiced slipping my new thing in and out of the little slot. I put on a baggy suit, one of the ones Barry called dyke clothes, tied my hair into a ponytail, filled my pockets with change, bills, and keys, and went out.

I caught my reflection walking jauntily down the street alongside me. I stopped, concerned. Hadn't I embraced this male posture rather too easily? What if the spell or curse, or whatever it was, didn't wear off? What if I was now, really and forever, a man? I'd have to buy all new clothes, I thought, and what would I tell my mother? And Barry? I found a pay phone to call him, not sure what I would say. When he didn't recognize my voice I decided to try a little experiment. I told Barry I was an acquaintance of his from college, I fabricated enough to convince him to meet me for a drink later. Besides lying, I wasn't sure what I was up to in my male/female mind. I was becoming used to my new dick, but underneath I remained uneasy.

I stopped at my usual newsstand for a paper. Al didn't recognize me, and he seemed suspicious that I knew his name. "Who sent you?" he asked. I pretended not to hear; I was distracted by the leering women posed on *Penthouse* and *Hustler*, positioned coyly behind the packets of Life Savers. It was then that I decided to buy condoms. Could a girl with a temporary penis impregnate another girl? I wished now that I had read the fine print on the back of the offer; I never read directions, Barry was always after me for that, he said it was girlish. I tossed down three bits for the paper. Old Al had been eyeing me; he gave me a knowing wink, in reference to the girlie mags, I guess. I folded the *Times* under my arm and ducked into the subway. I hadn't liked Al's wink; it was conspiratorial, hinting heavily at the do-to, done-to sexual dynamic.

Oh, but the subway! I went into sexual overload: women were everywhere. They were beautiful; even the plain ones held hope and destiny between their legs. Girls girls girls, tantalizing, alluring, goddesses going to work. Through a blouse I spied the curve of a breast, and there, a calf pumped from an achingly high heel; another woman had hips that could swallow me. I felt powerless; the stirrings were too much. I ran off the train at the next stop, careful to hold the paper in front of me as I climbed up the steps; I didn't know how much it took to fire the new thing off.

On the avenue more dames bustled along, oblivious to my pain and need. I was a kid loose in a candy store without enough change; I was new at this male game and it didn't look as if I'd become a pro anytime soon. And why had I started talking like a *film noir* antihero, a Sam Spade or Philip Marlowe? Pulp private eyes had once been my dream heroes, back when I was gawky and hopeful. Had I internalized Robert Mitchum, the tough-guy poet? Was this the sort of guy I wanted to be? I walked for blocks, feeling myself frequently. I'm not sure why. Perhaps I thought my male miracle might drop off.

It was a warm day in late spring. I sat on a park bench near Madison and Twenty-sixth to sort things out as the day drifted into nowhere. There had to be some meaning to this B movie I seemed caught in. I felt strangely agitated. If I'd still been a broad I'd have described myself as upset. It was then that I noticed the pink polish on my fingernails. I quickly went to a shop for remover. The salesgirl was pretty, so I said to her, "Sweetheart, marry me." She had the right smile, but her giggle was a disappointment; maybe I was maturing as a man. Barry had once said that all men were pigs. I'd tried to argue the point, asking if all women were, too. He'd said, "No, they're less in touch with themselves sexually."

I'd said, "So anyone who is in touch with themselves is a pig?"

Barry answered, "For lack of a better word, yes." To be honest, I'd have to say that right now I clearly was, for lack of a better word, a pig. I was on the other side of the sexual mystery and I didn't have a clue. There was only one thing I was sure of: I intended to use Barry to help me find a girl.

When we met for drinks I snowed him with college stories he had told me. He kept repeating that my face was familiar, though for the life of him he couldn't place it. I laughed. He liked me, I could tell by the way he nudged me when he told the joke about the old bull and the young bull. He bought drinks; I bought another round. I had a notion that Enigma was really on to Barry. Now that I looked at him man-to-man, immune to his drop-dead looks and without the sexual intrigue that usually stood between us, he was kind of nasty. Had I ever actually talked to Barry?

Over dinner I confided that I was new in town and overwhelmed by all the beautiful but unavailable women. Barry sympathized and said, "A man need never feel alone in this city."

"How about you?" I asked. "Seeing anyone, yourself?"

"Well, yeah, sort of." The poor guy actually looked embarrassed.

"You had a misunderstanding?" I ventured to guess. Barry shook his head.

"She thinks there's another woman?" I pushed. Barry squinted. I had to be careful. "Well, what else could it be?" I added.

"Myrna makes things up," he said. "She imagines I'm flirting with someone at my office."

"And you're as innocent as baby puke, right?" I said coolly.

"With the office girls I am. . . ." Barry answered, curling his lip.

I lowered my voice. "So you could turn me on to a babe, I mean tonight?"

Barry studied me for a few seconds. I thought the jig was up, he had figured me out. He said, "I don't know who you are."

"We used to know each other, remember?" I said.

"Yeah, college." Then he got this cocky expression on his face and, lowering his voice, came in close. "I *am* seeing another woman. I mean, Myrna is the one but I can't quite shake Delores. It's been going on for years."

I had a sudden desire to smash Barry in the face, but I kept myself in check and ordered us another drink. "Does Delores have a friend?" I asked.

"She might have." He grinned.

Barry found a phone and called Delores. She said to come on over. The night had turned foggy and the dark city streets were slick. I was all knots inside as the cab sped downtown, over the Brooklyn Bridge into the Heights, where Delores kept a swell apartment with a classy view. I was impressed, and Delores was beautiful, a real curvy knockout. I kind of wanted to smash her one, too, but I was also smitten, especially when her hand brushed mine as she handed me a drink and I took in her subtle perfume. I heard the swish of silk.

"Barry says you're from out of town," she purred.

"Yeah, he's a stranger, doll," Barry cut in, "and he's looking for company." Was I mistaken or was Barry starting to talk like a private eye, too? I felt like Sam Spade caught in a sticky situation; the bad guy had the girl and I half expected to find the Maltese Falcon perched on her mantelpiece. Somehow I was supposed to play the hero. My head was spinning again, so I took a tug on my drink.

I found refuge in Delores's big brown peepers, then looked down, kind of Bogart-shy. "A guy can get lonely." I twitched. "It's not a crime."

"Anyone can get lonely," she said.

"Even a woman like you?" I asked.

"Especially a woman like me," she said.

I didn't know what I was saying when the words came

tumbling out: "Why does someone like you settle for half the man?" As I spoke I moved a step closer. She did, too.

"Hey, what the hell is going on here?" said Barry, coming toward us with a menacing swagger. Barry was bigger than I, and I got the sinking sensation that the punch I meant to land on his jaw was about to knock on mine instead. I had the idea that time was slowing; a kind of lethargy engulfed me. I glanced at Delores. Her expression seemed fearful and somehow kindly. I was confused. Sneering, Barry said, "What's your game, mister?" He was closing in. I realized now that the lethargy I felt was fear.

I didn't have time to think before Barry made his move, but he'd had a lot to drink and wasn't too steady on his feet. He tripped over a striped pouf that stood between us. As he tried to regain his balance I let him have it, hard as I could, wham! Right in the kisser. Barry swayed, then sort of crumpled on the rug in front of Delores. "He's out," I said, hoping he wasn't dead.

"You don't know how much he deserved that," said Delores, looking down at Barry.

"I think I have an idea," I said, dropping my eyes.

Delores said she liked my style. She asked what hotel I was in. I told her I was borrowing an old friend's apartment. I was thrilled when she said, "Let's get out of here."

I couldn't resist. "Where to?"

Delores blinked her deep brown wells, "Your place, silly." She smiled.

It was getting late, dangerously close to the midnight hour, but I felt the destiny of this strange day was finally within my grasp. I was close to possessing the secret. It would be my hermaphroditic fate to resolve the carnal war that began with Eve's apple and Adam's erection. I stood on the threshold. My longing and desire knew no bounds as I opened the door to my apartment and led Delores inside.

We wasted little time; Delores was as on fire as I was. I could hardly restrain my ardor. My proud new member was getting ahead of me. I wanted to undress Delores slowly, to savor the moment, to kiss her neck and touch every part of her. Ahead of myself, I wanted to taste her, to know her inside out. When she kneeled down and opened my zipper I felt the first involuntary thrust. It came rushing like a wave; I pulled Delores up toward me and held her hips close, pressing against the fabric of her skirt, feeling her warm flesh beneath. Then the dam broke and the river flowed. I had committed the greatest folly a woman knows in a man: I had come too soon. Soon, I said to myself in despair—I was a week early! I wasn't certain if she knew. "Delores," I said, "excuse me a minute."

I ran to the bathroom. This was the sort of stunt a sixteen-year-old would pull, I thought; not even Philip Marlowe could have suaved his way out of this one. After about ten minutes Delores knocked gently on the door. "Are you all right?" she asked. "Yes," I said gratefully. "Yes!"

I opened the door and moved Delores firmly toward the bed. I was amazed by my quick recovery. We lay down. Delores was eager; she smiled and whispered in my ear that I was wonderful. "New equipment," I whispered back as I opened her satin bra. I was calm now. I felt celebratory, ready to make myself one with Delores; this had to be my mission, I would plunge into her as deeply as I could. "Ah, Delores," I said as I removed her panties.

Now Enigma sashayed into the bedroom. She rubbed her fur along Delores's leg, then sat and stared at me in the semi-darkness. I had a moment's doubt and looked back, vexed. Delores pulled me toward her; she was wide open. "I can't stop now," I told myself as I felt her steaming wetness. "Ah, Delores," I moaned as Enigma let out a low growling lament, and the clock struck twelve.

Jackie O Reads *Story of O* and Wonders About Having Her Own Penis for a Day

LYN LIFSHIN

If a woman like O, into fashion and
interior design, a woman who wore
only the best Parisian clothes,
knew Ionic columns from Doric ones,

could have let such flesh
whales do what they did in every part
of her, mouth, vagina, and even
what must have become an incredibly

rash red asshole. A woman who read
and knew art couldn't be too unlike her.
It's not that she was an environmentalist
out to save some thrashing dying male

manatee or spotted owl and so let
them plunge into the cove of her

skin. She wonders if that's why O put
an owl mask over her head and let her

self be led by a chain? Not that she wasn't
led, Jackie sighs. And led on. She might
as well have had a ring filed thru her labia,
been a slave. She's felt branded, had her

own masks, did what she did for love, too,
her hands tied. Like O, her clothes, her
inner feelings and architecture are
her main intrigues. She tries to imagine

herself in O's body. The best way to get
close would be with a penis of her own,
just for a day. She shudders, knows O did
like women too, and her name's even in O's writing,

another pleasure they could share. Her penis
would be like a massive horse between her
legs, that thick warmth that sweeps
her off her feet and won't cheat on

her but let her hips roll with a
deep sensuous pitch, a half ton of snort
and leather after so many years of riding
that giant phallus,—often better than,

well, she won't get into *that.* On the night
something starts to grow inside her she whispers
Penis over and over in her breathy soft
way as if to make the word flesh until

skin jolts up, a dick big as an amaryllis,
a favorite flower of O's she's heard, sure to
lure her to a château in Roissy. "How," Jackie
shivers, "could O, anonymous and cool as me, not be

open to such a stalk." This wouldn't be the first
big O in her life but maybe this time it will stand
for orgasm she pants as she imagines plunging into O
passionately as if she was redecorating the whole

White House. This time she'd have a bone, not
a home of her own, O the sheath she'll fill
as well as she has the others tho this one's
not of black linen or silk but moist as her own mouth.

She'll canter and trot, ride O as she would a stallion.
Afterward, they'll curl in the dark, maybe talk
about O.J., wish Nicole had *her* own penis,
her gun, stick, spear, sword, knife that could if it had to

slice another lap sausage, only they'd use French words,
come up with a barrage as they talked about men
who liked to roam. Then they'd go out shopping,
have snails, eager to rush back to that elegant space

with lush interiors to play with, redo a little more
than just the rooms

Same Difference

CATHARINE LUMBY

Rose woke unusually early, with an odd Christmassy sort of feeling in her stomach. The sliver of sky between the high-rises outside her window was still a fragile oyster gray, but the traffic below was already backed up.

She shut her eyes again and lay in bed listening to the jazz of gratuitous male aggression. Revving engines. Tire squeals. The odd insult.

"Fuck you."

"No, fuck *you*."

And car horns. Endless bloody car horns.

What were these guys *thinking*? Had they all taken some secret boys-only physics class in which a scientist explained the traffic-mobilizing properties of noise? Or was the aggro simply hormonal? A standard-issue dick thing? "Would you like some repressed rage with that, sir?" Rose snorted.

Before she had a chance to get down and wallow in her contempt, something darted in front of her train of thought. Something that looked remarkably like a penis. Startled, she sat up and checked the clock. Eight already. She'd better get moving.

Like most journalists, Rose hated getting out of bed before ten. But today was her first day in a new position at her job. What's more, she was sitting on one of the best stories of her life. Or was just about to be.

Rose rolled out of bed, pulled on a robe, booted up her computer, and began to experiment with write-offs. "The Phallus Analysis—Rose Sélavy Files an Inside Report on the State of the Signifier." She read it out loud. Too pretentious. She tried again. "A Day in the Life of a Dick—Rose Sélavy Penetrates the Male Psyche." Nah. Too cute. "Masculinity After Feminism: Rose Sélavy Assesses the Leaning Tower of Penis." Too . . . *Men's Health*. She bit her thumb. The doorbell rang.

It was Federal Express. Rose scrawled her initials on the proferred sheet and retreated into her bedroom to tear open the modest rectangular package she'd been expecting.

There on a bed of tissue paper lay the most perfect male member she'd ever seen. Pink, plump, and about four and a half inches long, it practically glowed with health. It was so beautiful, so innocent, that she was seized with an irrational desire to stroke it.

Reminding herself that she needed to maintain professional distance, Rose set down the box, opened the instruction book, and read:

PENIS™ INSTRUCTIONS

Standard Heterosexual Model (U.S. Patent No. 6,945,776)

Patriarchal Privileges Fully Included

One Size Fits All

Please read this booklet carefully to familiarize yourself with the operation of your Penis™ and with the Limited Warranty.

WARNING: Please note that the consumption of alcoholic beverages may seriously impair the performance of your Penis™. Phallocraft Incorporated bears no responsibility for psychological damage to the wearer resulting from malfunctions.

Yeah, yeah, yeah. Rose flipped the page and skimmed the rest of the laborious text. Jesus. They made it sound like you needed a Ph.D. in biology to operate something half the idiots on the planet were wandering around with. Trust male engineers to make the male organ sound more complicated than it was. Rose glanced over at the vast array of feminist literature spilling off her bookshelf. All she needed to know about this baby was in there.

She tossed the instructions aside and picked up the dick by its scrotum. It was lighter than she'd expected—softer and smaller, too. Arranged in the shape of a comma, in fact, the whole ensemble, from head to balls, sat perfectly in her palm. Rose gave it a casual squeeze and watched it grow slightly, unraveling like a coiled jelly snake in the warmth of her hand.

Then she opened her bathrobe and tried it on. It took to her instantly, like a warm sock.

Rose checked the results in the mirror. The penis hung

meekly enough between her legs, but its effect on the rest of her body was dramatic. Her breasts had shrunk and hardened. Her hips had narrowed and straightened. Her waist was wider. Her shoulders were broader. And there was something else she couldn't quite put her finger on—a pleasurable sense of solidity. A feeling of being grounded. As if her center of gravity had shifted. Rose tucked her new addition into a pair of extra-large underpants, threw on a suit, and headed off to the gym.

⚜

"Have a good one, buddy."

Was it her imagination, or had the normally surly guy at the desk just winked at her when he tossed her a towel? The brief walk from her apartment building to the local sports club had already confirmed one of Rose's deepest suspicions about men. The doorman, who had never so much as grunted at her before, now exchanged pleasantries about the weather. The guy at the local deli had *smothered* her bagel in cream cheese. And some perfect stranger waiting in line tried to engage her in a full-fledged conversation about basketball. It was just as she'd thought: a penis was a passport to a secret and vastly influential club.

In the pool, Rose shouldered her way through the water with uncharacteristic ease. She got a kick out of passing the young woman swimming in the lane to her right, and an older man in the lane to her left. She was so consumed with the competition, in fact, that before she knew it she'd finished her mile and was headed for the locker room.

A weird sour smell, like wet washing left overnight in a

basket, hung about the room. Rose glanced around. A pudgy middle-aged man struggled silently and sweatily with his underwear while a muscle-bound jock watched the battle with faint amusement. He caught Rose's eye and grinned conspiratorially.

"What's up, man?"

Rose flushed at the unexpected attention and searched for a suitably macho response. "Yo"? "Hey there"? "How's it hanging?" "Fuck you"? What was the point of the question anyway? Before she could decide, however, her bulky new friend was heading for the showers.

Rose tagged along behind him in the direction of the steam, where she found, to her surprise, not individual shower stalls but a large tiled room full of noisy, naked men swapping soap and jokes.

Rose had never taken a shower in public before. She slipped under the only spare nozzle and turned on the spray, hoping no one was watching. Her friend the jock was soaping his enormous buttocks under the next shower along. Directly across from her two middle-aged guys with identical paunches were discussing the credibility of Demi Moore's breasts. Next to them a much older bloke was standing with his eyes closed, letting the water beat down on his face. None of them acknowledged her presence. All of them were naked.

Rose figured she ought to lose her Speedos. At least it *seemed* the way to go. She turned her attention to the tight wet knot at the top of her trunks. How did these things work?

After a few nervous and increasingly unprofitable minutes, Rose turned to face the wall and began fumbling violently with the drawstring. Eventually the fabric around the knot gave and her bathers sailed straight to her ankles. She turned to face her fellow shower jocks.

She sensed that all eyes were on her. Something was wrong. Despite herself—and she knew this was a suicidal gesture—she glanced down. Her penis had vanished.

Rose looked harder. Her frantic eyes eventually located a small blue acorn.

She looked up. Her jock friend was now staring openly at her groin. Bravely, Rose returned his gaze. A penis the size of an eggplant dangled between his legs. Male camaraderie seemed strangely absent from this exchange. Rose shut off the shower and retreated gratefully to the sanctuary of her towel.

🎎

Rose was still organizing her desk when her new editor, Jack Pullen, put his head around her cubicle divider.

"How you doing so far?" Pullen winked and effected a little golfer's swing, which he punctuated with a click of his tongue. "Getting any yet?"

Rose looked up, confused. Getting any what? Pussy? Golf? Work done? She shrugged.

"Sure, plenty."

Pullen appeared to like the answer. "There you go. Come for a wander with me, buddy. I want to kick something around."

Rose followed him into the corridor. His office was to the right, but he took a sudden left. Where was he going? Rose's pulse quickened.

She sensed he was taking her somewhere special. A privileged room, perhaps, explicitly designed to exclude women.

A place *real* business was done. Pullen swung into the men's room and, with a sharp intake of breath, Rose followed.

Toilet stalls lined one wall, and a long stainless steel trough ran the length of the other. Pullen planted himself in the middle of the latter. Rose realized she'd never actually thought through the practicalities of networking in a toilet. She'd vaguely imagined some kind of luxurious antechamber furnished with leather couches and reclining lounge chairs. Or maybe a room with a desk and a couple of chairs. Even a mirror, for Christ's sake, where men could stand together and pretend to adjust their ties. But the only communal thing in this men's room was a steel trough you pissed in. And Pullen was making himself comfortable.

"Look, you're new here and I thought you ought to know about this sexual harassment trend. What do you make of it?" Pullen unzipped his trousers and retrieved his dick. Rose watched intently, the way she'd watch a spider she was trapped with in a small room. Hands on hips, he rocked back on his heels slightly and paused, obviously waiting for her response.

Rose thought it best to follow suit. She unzipped her own pants, located her penis and cautiously brought it out. Apparently satisfied with this answer, Pullen continued.

"Because, if you want my view, it's the last straw. We may as well just hand them our balls on a plate. First they want our jobs. Then they want to bring their kids to work with them. Now they want to turn us into a bunch of fucking priests. Jesus Christ. They'll be forcing us to hire fat chicks next." His hands still firmly clamped on his hips, Pullen leaned back even further and released a gushing stream of urine. He glanced across at Rose. She pointed her penis valiantly at the urinal but nothing was happening.

She concentrated. She thought of running water. She thought of how much she actually needed to go. But her urethra refused to respond. The urination signal remained stalled somewhere between her brain and her bladder.

After what seemed like half an hour of noisy voiding, Pullen shook his penis vigorously and zipped up. Rose remained rooted to the spot.

Pullen looked at her sideways. She gave her penis a feeble shake and sneaked it back into her pants. They both knew the truth.

"See you in conference." Pullen was looking at her with what she took for thinly veiled contempt. Rose was sweating now—this men's-room networking was tougher than she'd imagined.

"See you there." She waited till Pullen was safely out of sight and slipped quietly into a stall.

🏃

Straight after conference, Rose retired to the pub with a bunch of the guys—a Friday custom among the male editors. Rose had never been to one of these lunches before, though she'd often sat at her desk picking at a sandwich and imagining the lengthy discussions they were having on doing women down.

As much as she hated the smoky, beer-sodden atmosphere of the Bear's Armpit, she couldn't pass up the opportunity to take notes on this particular bunker of male power. So she settled back with a greasy burger, French fries, and a light beer, ready for a frank briefing on current strategies for maintaining Western patriarchy.

Today, however, her interlocutors seemed oddly out of sorts. After a relatively cheery chat about hair loss and low sperm counts they moved quickly on to a discussion of prostate cancer and high cholesterol. By midday, biological catastrophe had given way to socioeconomic disaster. The most optimistic topics included the inability of late capitalism to support a middle class, the demise of print media, and the imminence of mass structural unemployment. It was only as the morbid group waded into their third round of drinks, in fact, that the subject of masculine power reared its head. And that was when things got teary.

To her horror, Rose found herself almost sympathizing with Mitchell the sports editor, a monosyllabic meathead whom she'd always pegged as a wife beater. It turned out his wife *had* left him the previous year after he taped a football game over a three-hour special on Friedrich Nietzsche she'd been saving. Mitchell was convinced it was only a temporary absence.

"I'm only learning the basics—chips, chops, and sandwiches. She'll be back when she gets this philosophy thing out of her system." He drained his beer and torched up another Marlboro.

Rose's rational mind was telling her that Mitchell was a sexist asshole who deserved everything he got. But up this close she kept losing the big picture in the paltry details. Mitchell's hokey beige cardigan, for instance. His phenomenally bad haircut. The alcoholic gaps in his neural network. Instead of setting him straight, she found herself offering to buy him a scotch.

When she returned Mitchell was crying happily into the dregs of her beer. He demolished the scotch in one gulp, exhaled an alcoholic endearment in her face, and threw his arm heavily around her shoulder in a matey embrace.

And that's when it happened. With no warning—not a flicker of desire, even a hint of conscious mental activity—Rose got her first erection.

At first she thought her penis was simply shifting in a natural response to a change in her sitting position. But then she noticed an odd new pressure building in her underpants. The crotch of her trousers seemed to be shrinking. Her groin felt hot. She looked down. Her cock was crushed up against her abdomen, bulging against her pants in a most undignified manner. She looked up.

No one had noticed, thank Christ.

But how long before they did? She couldn't leave the table like this. Rose slid her hand surreptitiously into her pocket and squeezed the shaft of her cock through her underpants. Wrong move: that felt good.

She withdrew her hand and concentrated on losing her erection. She thought of deflating balloons. She thought of wilting flowers. She thought of crushed kittens. Crushed *kittens?* She felt her dick again. Hard as a rock. Christ. It was totally out of control.

Rose shifted helplessly under the sweaty weight of Mitchell's matey arm.

What had brought her erection on? And why was Mitchell sitting so close to her? Was he making a pass at her? *Jesus.* Was her penis making a pass at him? And why was she having such homophobic thoughts?

Rose took another look at Mitchell, taking time to register his ruined blotchy face and his low-IQ stare. She thought long and hard about placing her tongue in his fermented mouth. To her relief she felt her dick subside.

🐦

Slightly drunk, the burger lingering in her stomach like a stone, and terrified of meeting Pullen at the urinal again, Rose spent the afternoon staring at her blinking cursor. By six P.M. she was ready to pack it in. She hadn't written a word all day.

The bar was already humming with the Friday crowd when she arrived. Rose didn't come here normally. She looked around. Mitchell and a couple of the boys were still hunkered down over their drinks in the corner. She found a stool at the opposite end of the bar, ordered a vodka and tonic, and fished out a computer printout of her scattered notes.

"You work at the newspaper?" A young woman was fixing her with an unnaturally bright smile. Rose nodded and returned to the sheaf of paper in front of her.

"Are you a writer?" Rose looked up, vaguely annoyed. The woman was still staring at her.

"Yes. I'm a writer." Rose paused, narrowed her eyes, and pointedly returned to her work.

"Cool."

Cool? Rose finished her drink and set the glass down on the bar. The barman caught her look and sidled over.

Before she could open her mouth, though, her new friend had already piped up. "I'll have a double Cointreau on ice. With milk." She turned to Rose. "Thanks. I'm Debbie."

With a start, Rose realized she was being hit on. By a stranger in a bar. While she was trying to work.

Rose had a game plan for this situation. Any chauvinist fucker who assumed she was available simply because she was sitting alone in a bar could piss off. But this chauvinist fucker was a woman.

Rose took a second look at her tormentor. She looked like most other women who flirted with the enemy. Blond. Anorexic. Too much makeup. Rose swallowed her second vodka and ordered another.

Later, in the cab, she tried to recall their conversation. It seemed as if Debbie had done all the talking. Now she was directing the driver to take them to her place. Rose knew what came next. Her palms began to sweat. She was nervous.

Rose had been to bed with girls before. She almost never had sex with men. But this was different. For one thing, Debbie was nothing like the girls Rose normally slept with . . . she was a *girl* girl. And for another thing, there were three of them to think about here: Debbie, Rose, and the thing in Rose's pants.

It seemed eager enough. She could feel it swelling contentedly against her left thigh. But they were barely in the door of Debbie's apartment when it changed its mind.

Within minutes Debbie had Whitney Houston oozing from the CD player and a sticky Cointreau-laced tongue in Rose's mouth. As her hand moved toward Rose's crotch, Rose felt her penis begin to retract. She caught Debbie's wrist and tried to think of something sexually inspiring. What turned straight men on? She tried to remember. A tatty poster of Farrah Fawcett-Majors in a swimsuit flashed into her mind. She checked her weapon. No response. She tried again. Claudia Schiffer topless. Nothing. Elle MacPherson with no undies. Zero. Naomi Campbell bent double over a Ferrari. Not a flicker. What next? Debbie had freed her hand and was circling exploratively around Rose's groin. Jesus.

Rose excused herself and located the bathroom. She locked the door, fished the traitor out of her underpants and stared at it accusingly. It looked normal enough. She rubbed it experimentally and it expanded. She rubbed it some more. Hmm. Maybe if she . . . Debbie banged on the door. "Whatcha doing in there?"

Her erection fled.

Three awkward minutes later, Rose followed suit.

⚥

It was after one A.M. when Rose pushed open the frozen window in her living room. It was snowing quite heavily outside now, but she leaned her body most of the way out to watch the dick drop. It sailed quickly down the twelve stories to the street below. She could just make it out—a small pink comma against the white. A dog began to sniff it. The woman walking the dog bent down, curious.

Rose shivered and pulled her head back inside. Good riddance.

Her anger began to subside. She began to feel a little more in control. A bit more like her old self. Silly to let a *penis* get to her in the first place. It hadn't told her anything, after all. Just what you'd expect from a male organ—it wasn't about to hand over the secrets of patriarchal power to a woman.

Rose snorted. She had work to do. A penis to document. Patriarchs to expose. Masculinity to deconstruct. Her writer's block was dissolving at last. She undressed, pulled on a robe, and booted up her computer. She began to write.

DIANE DI MASSA

I would finally understand once and for all WHY this raw turkey neck makes men superior! (Gosh, was I CLUELESS! Oh, I do apologize for all those nasty cartoons!) THEN . . . I'd jerk off while looking at . . . ANYTHING! Then the real fun would begin; I'd run and show it to all my dyke pals who have never really seen one up close. I'd put it in a hot dog roll, let my cat smell it, see if it fit in my underwear, pose with it, and maybe have it hollowed out and use it for a change purse or a flag holder. I'd do jumping jacks on the bed naked and make my girlfriend retch. I suppose I'd measure it, maybe do a painting with it; I'm sure since I'm Italian I'd have a really huge one so I'd TRIP over it, maybe even JUMP ROPE with it. I'd get some fag to suck it, compare it to my favorite dildo, and see if I could stick it up my own butt. I'd consider my period coming out of it and wonder what the pad would look like. A little cotton bucket? Then, at the end of the big day, I'd look at it and just feel grateful that my brain wasn't in there.

Jook Sing and the Dragon

AVA CHIN

Reporter: Are you going to stay in Hong Kong and be famous, or are you going to try the United States?

Bruce Lee: I'm going to do both because I have already made up my mind that in the United States, I think something of the Oriental, I mean the true Oriental, should be shown.

It was detachable and independent. Her mother would say it had a mind of its own, like her, except at times it didn't think so much as be very sensitive and hide in the couch when it was feeling small.

At her desk, she typed for long periods of time, several hours in fact, and she often forgot about it (though it was always in the back of her head, not unlike her mother's words, "A man is like a cold!" or "If he's like your father, forget it!"). Cups of half-drunk tea would pool around her computer and clicking fingers. She was a quick drinker and a swift typist.

Sometimes it would disappear for days, decades, even centuries, and she would slam objects around her desk and kitchen. She would talk on the phone while fixing her hair and pretend that she didn't care. She'd eat a lot of chocolate or throw an elaborate dinner. Sometimes she was glad it was missing: she didn't have to worry about it popping out at the wrong time (like when her mother was over, or when the occasional lover jumped out of bed at the odd hour to brew some coffee). Mostly though, she'd wait on the couch, hoping it would appear.

When she first met it, it was very proud and puffed up. It was eager to take on lots of work, even more than it could handle. Many things went over its head, like its inability to pronounce her name, so it opted for the miscellaneous "Hey you!" whenever possible. She tried to teach it English, but it staunchly refused. Frustrated, she'd sometimes accuse it of being unwilling to adapt to a new country and culture. Secretly, it labeled her an assimilationist.

Since she was adamant about proper usage and vocabulary, and it looked down on her as an ABC or jook sing (meaning "overseas Chinese," or, more literally, "piece of bamboo closed on both ends"), they communicated mostly through hand gestures and a veil of hurt feelings. In actuality, it was only afraid of making a mistake.

The first time she brought home takeout, it idled over to the table. Rice steamed from her chopsticks. She noticed it getting very large and proud. It jumped over the edge of the carton like a diving board and plunged headlong into the egg foo-yung. For a moment it shivered, as if it had landed in the ocean it had so recently crossed. It blanched at such an

American bastardization of a good meal, but secretly, it didn't think the food was half bad.

One night she came home from a date to find all of its unemployed friends surrounding the laser disc player singing karaoke. Beer bottles and cigarette ash dotted the floor. Open containers of Chinese food had spilled onto the rug, and the picture of her mother had fallen off its hook. It wore her scarf around its head as it waved from the couch.

The next selection was a particularly tempting Hong Kong love song which it dedicated to her. Back in Guanzhou it was regarded as something of a singer. A big shot from Hong Kong had even offered it a contract, but it held out for too long for more money and eventually they decided to sign the son of a top executive.

It had barely finished the ending notes when she threw the last of its friends out, shouting something about mah-jongg downtown before she shut the door. It didn't seem to realize she was angry, just dove into the opening bars of "Unchained Melody" thinking to impress her. Its English was getting quite good.

Bruce spent time working on an idea about the adventures of a Shaolin priest who used martial arts skills against outlaws of the Old West with the working title "The Warrior," later known as Kung Fu.

The next morning her downstairs neighbor tacked a "No Chinese Menus Please" sign on the door while it was preparing for a jog. It shrank to the size of a dime. Though she searched in the closet, under the bed, and in the couch, it didn't resurface until two weeks later. Even then things weren't the same.

> Saloon Owner: Hey look! We got us a Chinaman here.
> David Carradine: You talking to me?

When she returned from work it was watching *Kung Fu* on TV. Carradine was fighting rednecks in the Wild West. She tried flipping the channels but it insisted on viewing the program.

"Why are you watching this? You'll only make yourself more depressed!" she argued, but the fight was one-sided, as it ignored her. She thought about making its favorite meal of Chinese sausage and rice, or even some fresh popcorn, but she thought that might be encouraging it, so she just left it alone to sulk.

> Reporter: Let me ask you about the problems you face as a Chinese hero in an American series. Have people come up to you in the industry and said, "We don't know how the audience is going to take an Asian lead?"
> Lee: The question has been raised. In fact, that is why "The Warrior" is probably not going to be on. . . . They think, business-wise, it's a risk.

By the third week it still hadn't moved from the sofa. Beer bottles and peanuts littered the floor. Its pallor was an uncommon gray.

"Look, I'm really sorry about your friends, but karaoke drives me crazy," she started. "Hey, what's the matter with you?"

She was confused when it didn't answer. Where was the tough, proud stance it had displayed so early on?

"Listen, you can sing me 'Unchained Melody' if you like. . . ."

But it remained tiny and unblinking on the couch, scratching its bottom. Silent, inconsequential, and very, very small.

"Why are you fulfilling a stereotype?" she screamed, throwing a pillow to get its attention. It pretended it didn't understand English and was engrossed in a commercial.

When the studio rejected Bruce from the role, he was angry and heartbroken. Not only was it his concept, but we had written the part for him.

Producer of *Kung Fu*

Sometimes it took long walks in the park, under the cover of cherry blossom trees. Muttering all the way. She didn't understand. She was an object of desire. An assimilated jook sing. She didn't have people making fun of her on the train. Teasing her for being geeky and short. People shouting, "What? What did you say? Speak English!" when she *was*. If there was an event involving Asians, it was targeted. If Japanese were blamed for stealing auto jobs, it was Japanese. If there was a Korean-and-Black conflict, people taunted it for being Korean. Vets approached it on the street with "I cut your brother in Vietnam!" Even white folks in the East Village sneered that it was driving up the rents. Worse still, its Asian female counterpart didn't seem to get it. Sometimes she even brought home Caucasian men!

Under the silhouette of the setting sun, it cried and thought of all the weight it was losing.

⏢

"Lookit," she said, her head blocking its view of the TV. "*Enter the Dragon* is on." *Dragon* was one of its favorite films. Flying kicks and razor punches. High-pitched screams and animalistic grace. But this time, even the presence of nunchakus didn't help. They were just another reminder of Bruce's castration by Hollywood. It sighed a little and drank another beer.

"Hmm," she said before returning to her desk. It was not long before her fingers began swiftly typing.

At work she leafed through notes and old journals. Paper and videotape. She made phone calls to experts in L.A. and Hong Kong. By the time she had enough to go on, the books had piled so high on her desk she couldn't see out the window. She met with editors to discuss angles and leads, and even impressed them with a detailed outline describing the scope and exacting clarity of her vision. ("How articulate she is! What good English she speaks," they thought.)

⏢

Years before, she and a boyfriend were in bed. He said, "I heard Japanese condoms are actually smaller than American ones." He paused briefly and phrased it as a question: "Do you think that means Asian men are smaller than American men?"

A small light glowed in his eyes as he fingered his member. An Asian woman was going to affirm his white American dick.

She said, "If you were doing it right, maybe you wouldn't be so preoccupied with size."

⚘

At five P.M., while it was channel-surfing, the door flew open and she beamed, triumphant, magazine in hand, yelling in her funny American accent. She said, "Look! Look!" in all the wrong tones, so it didn't understand and thought she was calling it "Mrs. ————!" Her Chinese was atrocious, but the light hit her hair in a pretty way and it thought the way her mouth moved to reach the high tones was attractive.

She pointed to the cover story. It was her by-line.

"Well, kudos for you," it muttered. Another triumph by jook sing woman. Suddenly the commercials became very interesting again.

"No, no," she protested. She suppressed the thought that maybe if it learned some vocabulary instead of going to the track or whatever it did when she wasn't around, then it wouldn't be so afraid of picking up an English newspaper and reading.

"Whatever," it said. "Let's see who they get when the revolution comes—working-class peon or bourgeois writer."

So she read aloud:

MOTION IN THE OCEAN OR
THE SIZE OF A BOAT?
DISMANTLING THE LITTLE MYTHS
SURROUNDING ASIAN MEN IN AMERICA:
"BRUCE LEE WAS 5´ 7˝ AND HE WAS THE
HOTTEST GUY IN HOLLYWOOD!"

That night while the sun set, they sat in the living room with the television on but the sound turned off. It candidly told her all about its hopes and fears, its arrival to America and broken career. She took notes without once correcting its grammar, her pen moving swiftly across the page, not wanting to miss a word.

Broken

A M Y   J E N K I N S

poor thing all i meant to do was play

but i got so excited and it all just

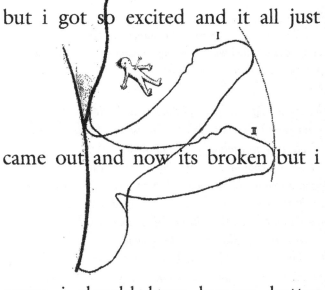

came out and now its broken but i

guess i should have known better

Ask Isadora

ISADORA ALMAN

Dear Isadora,

   If, by some bizarre stroke of nature, you were to suddenly find yourself, shall we say, newly anatomically endowed for just one day, what would you do?

This letter isn't signed. Most of them aren't. Mother Nature, is this from you? Genie, is this a lampless and bottleless freebie? Drat, this is probably one of those "philosophicals" where I get to expound a summation of all my thoughts and feelings on some profound subject in the space of no more than half an 800-word weekly column. Damned difficult, those. I'm more used to the usual dozens of letters of the How Best to Fit Prong A into Slot B variety. I prefer them to the relationship mazes with War and Peace–size casts, which I'm asked to unravel "without hurting anyone's feelings." Okay, a philosophical then. I haven't tackled one of those since I tried condensing the wisdom of ages on the workability of long-term monogamy.

⚭

I wake up one morning, stretch, grumble, scratch, and . . . Cheesus boom! What the hell is this? A woody, a piss hard-on, a morning erection. I know all about those. I've seen . . . oh, a goodly number. But this one isn't "borrowed"; it's mine, to do with what I want. Wow! So what *do* I want?

First, I'd play with it just a little, test the hydraulics—down, up, waggling it handlessly from side to side.

Then I'd pee, standing up—lifting the lid first, of course. Too bad this miracle happens in hometown temperate California, so I can't rush outdoors and write my name—or any other brief sentiments—in the snow.

I don't know if I could resist putting it through its paces right away, from neutral through mini–Mount St. Helens. Since there it would be, dangling tantalizingly between my legs and within easy reach of my soapy hands as I took my morning shower. Hold temptation at bay? Probably not. Carpe diem!

The decision to dress right or left would make itself as I slipped into loose slacks. Maybe, though, lacking a kilt, I'd just put on a skirt, no panties, and let it swing free, bumping provocatively against my inner thighs . . . maybe even against my knees if Nature were lavish in her bounty.

Off I'd run to the nearest purveyor of sexual supplies to buy an array of condoms, lubricants, and decorative accessories such as leather cock rings and rubber extensions. All this in the name of sexual science, of course, testing first . . .

um . . . hand complaints about the intrusiveness of such sexual adjuncts.

With new bag of toys in hand I'd make the rounds of my friends, male and female, gay, straight, and bi, interrupting them at their work if necessary to find out who wants to play with me and how.

Somewhere along my social roundelay I'd certainly have some photos taken, to commemorate the event.

When I had exhausted my creativity and that of all of my friends, and exhausted everything else in the process, I'd take myself home for some private reflection. I'd smooth some soothing lotion on my well-used surprise grant, perhaps address some soothing words of appreciation and affirmation to it as well, as we both lay down for some well-deserved rest. Should the soothing and the smoothing incite any sort of response (besides a wordless, sleepy thanks) this time I'd make sure to have a large mirror handy so that I could fall asleep to the sight of my bouncing breasts and bobbing balls in happy, satisfied conjunction.

Was it fun? Was it wonderful to have a dick for a day? Ask Isadora!

🛉

Well, out of space for this week's column. Pick up next week's newspaper, wherein I will discuss the possibilities of fitting Slot B onto Prong A.

MARYANNE DEVER

If I had a dick for a day, or any amount of time, I would stick it to my forehead and parade around the way its regular owners do.

Superdick

GRETEL KILLEEN

What am I going to do today?

First I think I'll sleep in, and not bounce my body out of bed till dawn. Then I'll kiss my wife upon her forehead and she'll have an orgasm while she sleeps.

Then I'll dress in something fabulous, probably white to match my teeth, and take Lightning, our purebred greyhound, for a jog. He'll keep up for the first twenty-two kilometers and I'll carry him on my back for the remaining forty-three.

Next I'll swim ninety-four lengths of our Olympic-sized lap pool and dry myself off with the fluffy white towel that Mummy gave me when I was born. As the soft fibers caress my evenly suntanned, muscular torso I'll think fondly of my mother and remind myself to call her at nine o'clock, as usual, just to say "I love you."

At six, after I've removed all excess facial and back hair,

I'll wake my magnificently beautiful, brilliant, generous, modest, caring, compassionate, contented, and wealthy wife. I'll notice what a striking resemblance she bears to Princess Diana, Mother Teresa, and that girl with the mouth in *Deep Throat* and then I'll wake her gently to discuss the synchronic elaboration of semiotic nuclei.

We'll have a lively, witty intellectual debate, agree about everything, and then perform advanced tantric sex while standing on our heads. My wife will have over two hundred orgasms, and I won't have any because satisfying my wife is satisfaction enough and instead I'll embrace her and cry with joy.

After that my darling will resume her slumber; I'll kiss her again, sweetly, upon the forehead. She'll have another orgasm while she sleeps and I'll go to find the Filipina maid who's so much like a member of the family that we don't even pay her.

Spontaneously I'll give the maid the whole morning off (because that's the sort of whimsical, impulsive, impetuous, lovable guy that I am) and I'll lend her fifteen bucks, at a very reasonable rate, so she can buy her family of seventeen some food and feel better about her mother's sudden death and father's emergency quadruple bypass. Then she'll, of course, ask how she can possibly repay me and I'll smile my engaging, roguish, charismatic grin, say "Think nothing of it," give her a hug, and accidentally brush my hand upon her neat pert breasts, and oops again, down the curve of her tight bottom.

I'll take a moment to think about life and death and the poor people's needless suffering and thank God that I both look more and more distinguished as I age and that I have an enormous dick. Then I'll get my mobile and wake my secretary (who I suspect is extremely sexually attracted to me) and tell her to make emergency appointments for my prostate, piles, and crow's feet.

After that I'll slip into some neat, soft, white shoes and one of those barbecue aprons with the bosoms painted on it, and prepare a sumptuous gourmet breakfast for my dear, devoted, wealthy better half. Perhaps a sliver of imported grapefruit with natural bran flakes (not that she needs them because she's very, very regular) and freshly squeezed orange juice made with fruit from the specially imported tree that I planted from a seed the first time we kissed and that now stands tall and strong like our love, between the swing I crafted all by myself and the children's cubby where my wife and I sometimes make love because we are so young and carefree and overflowing with youthful joie de vivre and because we both have really gorgeous bodies, mine more gorgeous than hers.

I'll spoon-feed the goddess-wife as she soaks in the bubble spa, turn the jet on ever so gently, and smile with pride as she has another orgasm.

At 7:30 I'll go to wake our two brilliant and beautiful children, a girl who looks a bit like Kate Moss and Barbara Walters and a boy who looks just like Macaulay Culkin, with a little bit of Jean-Claude Van Damme. As usual I'll probably find them making their beds and folding their clothes, so I'll vacuum their rooms as we cuddle.

From 7:35 to 7:38 A.M. we'll bond; then I'll style and set my gorgeous wife's gossamer hair, iron the shoulder-padded business suit she made from her wedding dress, analyze the

Dow Industrials, feed the dog his homemade muesli, and help the kids shoot a 35mm school project on the subject of the average family.

At 7:45 I'll check my pores, then I'll realign the distributor of the little woman's vehicle, straighten her hemline, tongue-kiss her good-bye, give her another orgasm, and wave her off to her impressive career as a feminist, pacifist, futurist, humanist, catering delegate to the U.N., and part-time supermodel.

Meanwhile the gorgeous and gifted children will resolve the theory of relativity as it pertains to weight loss. Then they'll finish making their pâté, sprout, and organic wholemeal bread sandwiches, and quickly bake a tiramisù to raise funds for the Let's Help Those Less Fortunate Than Ourselves Club.

I'll say, "Hurry up, kids, time for school, we'll be late," and we'll laugh and laugh and laugh, and then at 7:48 I'll bundle the children into the new Jeep, tell them to try not to sit on the expensive leather seats, and then drive off really really fast to their nondenominational, noncompetitive, individual-oriented private school, where the teachers always comment on how clean and bright my kids' uniforms are.

I'll be fabulous. I'll be voted father of the year. I'll kick a ball around with the boys and skip rope with the girls; I'll exchange recipes with the principal; and, when the mothers try to chat with me, I'll be moody, strong, silent, and intellectual until I see some young mum in tears over her recent separation and I'll touch base with my inner female and notice just how much it hurts to see a fellow human being so lonely and so devastated, especially when she has such great tits.

I'll give her a warm hug and she'll have an orgasm.

At nine A.M. I'll head home and go to the john for a moment's peace and quiet that will take about an hour. I'll read my stars, browse the politics in *Playboy*, do the crossword in *The New York Times*, and write a haiku about real love on the back of the toilet door.

At 10:15 I'll coif my chest hairs, attach my ponytail, hop onto my Harley 1200 Wanker, hoon to work and park on the sidewalk (because I own the building, and that building, and that one over there), run up the stairs to the 147th floor, accept the applause as I enter the office, and get my Harvard-educated triple-degreed secretary to trim my nasal hairs, rub my neck, and apply my herpes ointment. When she's finished I'll give her the sack because she's put on weight.

From eleven to twelve I'll interview secretaries and select about seventeen for hot dates this week. And then I'll practice my putting.

At twelve my private trainer will arrive and we'll openly and lovingly share the problems he's having with his latest boyfriend. I'll pat him on the back in a fond yet affectionate way, and he'll have an orgasm.

At 12:55 I'll have nothing scheduled and so I'll fiddle with my dick.

At one I'll go to lunch with a group of high-powered, hard-going, wheeling and dealing world leaders and we'll tell tit-and-ass jokes. At two I'll use some insider info to destroy the lives of thousands in a Third World country. At 2:30 I'll arrange to have a guy who owes me $200 lose the use of his left knee; at three I'll spend a couple of grand on a table for a socialite charity ball; at 3:30 I'll find a cockroach with a broken leg, fix it, and watch it scamper away, so cute.

At 3:35 I'll learn to fly a fighter jet and discover the cure for cancer. At 3:45 I'll get my lawyer to visit my mistress in the fabulous apartment I bought for the one I had two before her. He'll give her the Rolex I bought in Bangkok and tell her to first move all her stuff from the apartment and then help the new girl move in.

At 4:17 I'll be interviewed by *Good Housekeeping* magazine, and I'll tell them how to remove lipstick from the natural fiber carpet without damaging your fingernails.

I'll meditate. I'll masturbate. I'll go to our farm just outside the city, kill a fatted calf with my own bare hands, and bring it home to cook for the family dinner. I'll stop by my therapist's on the way. She'll sit me down and tell me to close my eyes and imagine that I'm floating down a sun-dappled river. I'll close my eyes and imagine that she's stark naked and I've got a ten-foot cock and I'm doing it to her and she comes eight million times. And then I'll open my eyes and I'll pretend that I'm crying and she'll hug me, and I suspect she'll have an orgasm.

Then I'll go home with the cow and the Harley, stop on the way to hug a tree, and chop it down for firewood with my teeth.

At six I'll shop for the groceries at our local mall, pay cash and tip the chick with the lips, let her have an orgasm, and then wander over to the fruit department, where I like to rub myself against the watermelons and show them a really good time.

At 6:15 I'll play a set on the court, let my old school friend beat me, be offered my own record-rating TV talk show, and pick the kids up from their computer program-ming/philosophy/ballet/madrigal/advanced aeronautics class. And then we'll all go together to visit some randomly se-lected poor old stranger and bring great joy to his/her life.

At 6:30 I'll prepare the entrée, chop the vegetables, help the children with their homework, give myself a facial, and do the family accounts.

I'll massage my wife from seven till eight and suggest we make long and passionate love for a few minutes on the floor. She'll have an orgasm and I'll just relax as I wash and iron, then clean the toilets until the fifteen influential guests and their wives arrive.

We'll discuss politics, fine food, high finance, our years in Provence, and our cholesterol levels. I'll contribute gener-ously to the conversation, but only in Swahili or Latin; then I'll play the piano, perform a makeover on Ivana ex Trump, and dance the *Nutcracker Suite* in the nude until absolutely all the guests have had at least one orgasm.

At one or two I'll pay for all the limos to take everyone home; then I'll clear up, wash up, put the plates away, read *Ulysses*, write a chapter of my thesis on the history of the cro-cheted poncho, and finish knitting Jean-Claude Culkin's ski socks.

And then, at four, I'll do four million press-ups, sidle up to my wife, kiss her as she sleeps, give her another orgasm, roll over, think about all that I achieved today, fiddle with myself, and have the biggest orgasm anyone in the history of the entire world has ever, ever had.

Oh, I'll probably fake that orgasm.

(But I'll fake it better than anyone else.)

Hangin' with Sanjay

AMRUTA SLEE

The woman sitting at the bar at Marion's cannot take her eyes off me. Maybe it's the rakish line of my spirit-gum-and-false-hair mustache. Or the manly way I grip my gin and tonic. As long as it's not the Ace bandage—which was binding my chest and has now slipped to my waist, making lumps under my shirt—that holds her in thrall. I am unsure how to respond to her gaze.

"How should I look at women?" I ask Diane Torr, who is instructing me on being a man.

"Purposefully," she advises. "And look straight through them as well."

We are out on the town, Diane and I, dressed in suits, ties, and mustaches, with penises made out of cloth pinned to our underwear. Diane, who teaches Drag King workshops to women, has volunteered to be my escort. She is "Danny," a sleazy, middle-aged businessman; I am "San-

jay," a young dandy. She has told me to develop my character, know who he is in case I have to speak to anyone. I'm
prepared to talk about how I'm expected to take over my
family's import-export business, how I hold an MBA from
Harvard, and how much I like New York. So far though, I'm
just another jerk in a bar.

How different is it to be male? I've always thought of myself as boyish; I wear jeans a lot, like my hair short, and don't
go in for traditional femininity. My superficial conversion
didn't take long: it was a matter of finding a suit that fitted—
for which I turned to a slightly built male friend—putting a
bit of dark powder on my face, and gluing false hair to my
upper lip and a smidge below my lower. My hair is gelled
back. Dark-skinned women, Diane tells me, look more convincing as men than fair ones. And facial hair is an instant
male signifier. She tells me to choose an image. I want to look
like Keanu Reeves but alas, end up resembling Robert
Downey, Jr., in *Chaplin* instead. Diane winds an Ace bandage around my breasts and pulls it tight, a not unpleasant
feeling though a bit restrictive at first. Then we're ready to
make the "penis."

Mine is a modest size, fashioned out of wads of cotton
wool stuffed into a cone-shaped bandage. With a safety pin
I attach it to my underwear and strut around for a while.
"How does it feel?" Diane asks, the anxious den father.
Weirdly, I don't even notice it; it is ineffectual and limp, but
I'm told it's hugely important to my new male psyche. When
men get fitted for suits they're asked how they "dress," that
is, whether their dick hangs to the left or the right. This is
what I want to experience, the "How's it hangin'?" cama-

raderie of men; but my cotton-wool penis simply lies in the middle of my pants like a sanitary pad. I might need balls to push it forward, but we don't bother making those.

In my apartment, I watch Diane pace up and down as Danny and try to imitate her. "Sit further back in the chair," she instructs. "Take up space." "Place things more firmly." "Curl your fists." "Less smiling—and don't touch your face." Masculinity comes down to flinging myself onto the sofa, legs wide apart, and looking around as though I own the place.

Diane tells me the story of how she got started in drag. One night she dressed up as a man for some photos, and when the shoot was over she went to an opening at New York's Whitney Museum wearing her "Danny" costume. As she stood in the corner sipping a beer, a woman approached her and tried to pick her up. She remembers this as highly embarrassing and also recalls that the woman spoke to her in a way she would never have spoken to another woman. "She made herself vulnerable to me." In response, Diane confined herself to nodding and brusque answers. "The way I was behaving," she says, "was probably typically macho stuff. Just sort of 'Oh yeah?', the way some men look at you with that air of bemused tolerance."

Since I suspect many women have thought, after passing another wolf-whistling twit, "If I were a man, would I have to put up with this?" Diane's anecdote is instructive. Men get hassled in public spaces too. But as I climb into Sanjay's clothes I'm hoping there will be some discernible differences in the way the sexes are treated, some validation of all the complaints I've mentally filed over the years.

The first news is that men's clothes are better made and more comfortable than women's. My suit is warm and snug. It also provides me with a feeling of safety; dressed in it I feel I'm shrouded from being spoken to. Yet leaving the apartment is nerve-racking. What if I'm bashed for being too effeminate? I work on my swagger. What if no one even notices? What if (horror!) they laugh?

⚭

My first stop is New York's "Little India" on Sixth Street, in the East Village. Here guys who look something like Sanjay hawk restaurant leaflets. As a woman I've often been subjected to a proprietary gaze along this stretch—"Here's one of 'our' girls"—and I'm keen to see how Sanjay will be treated. Diane and I linger outside restaurants, but we rate no interest until an Indian family wanders by. The women don't look my way but the older man in the group does, and he nods. It's like being in the Masons.

Being Sanjay makes me feel the way I do when I put on female drag, a tight dress and high heels: like a fraud ripe for unmasking. Simultaneously, I have a heightened awareness of how many feminine mannerisms I have unconsciously acquired over the years and how ill at ease I am without them. It's one thing to be boyish, knowing you can still enjoy the fun parts of being female; quite another to feel trapped inside a male body with all the attendant baggage of the enemy.

On the street I'm watching the faces of passersby for signs that I have "passed." Most men look over my head; they don't even see me anymore. More disconcerting is the way women seem to regard me as a predator. They drop their gaze when our eyes meet. Once in a while a woman who wants to have a second look at me will wait until we are parallel, then look sideways as she passes with a quick, furtive glance. I'm cut off from my community, alone in Man-land, and it feels yukky. "I'm a girl!" I keep wanting to say to the women.

Diane and I look for a place to eat, one that is dimly lit and uncrowded so I can win back my confidence. On the way there I'm thinking about each step I take—is it masculine enough? How masculine must it be? After all, Sanjay has a small build; would he take up the entire sidewalk like a beefy truck driver? I don't know what to do with my hands, or my shoulders either, what expression to wear on my face. And should I look at men or women?

We're in a restaurant. Diane eats like Danny, shoveling food in and moving her arm from the shoulder, eyeing women up and down with cold precision. Surely Sanjay, delicate flower that he is, would have better manners. Plus, the glue holding on my mustache has tightened into an itchy, irritating mass, and I'm scared to take a big mouthful of food in case it splits and falls in my soup.

Two women at the next table are amused by the scene. They say they thought we were gay. It dawns on me that Sanjay is experimenting with his sexuality. Perhaps he would like to go somewhere more . . . more *male*.

⚶

At the Stonewall Inn in the West Village I finally relax. It's fun to be a woman dressed as a man in a gay bar. The bartender is all attentive smiles; the man next to me, who has cleared a space, begins chatting. He doesn't notice how squeaky my voice is, or maybe he doesn't care. Glancing at the friends who have joined me, a man and a woman, he grimaces, saying, "Are they in love?" Back at my table I'm given the once-over by several pairs of eyes—something I would find irritating as a woman. But here the joke's on them, and I flirt audaciously, smiling and throwing my shoulders back. By now I've begun imitating gestures I've seen men make; standing with my foot on the bar rail, checking my inside breast pocket.

In a single night I could not hope to get a real sense of what it's like to be male. Although my male self *is* more confident, I didn't get to do the thing I most envy about men's lives—walk around with my shirt off on a hot summer day. No one called me sir, nobody challenged me to a fight or offered me entry to a secret society; and writing this, I know my expectations of what men do, who they are, sound like a cliché from the 1950s. At the Stonewall and on East Sixth Street there were small signs of different treatment, but no sudden bestowal of privilege.

I wish I could always walk down a street without being scrutinized. Or that I could go to a bar and flirt with people I find attractive and not be harassed. I don't want the penis, or the facial hair that startles me every time I touch my chin or look in the mirror. I wish men, and women too, had created less cartoonish identities for themselves so we could all relax a bit.

Across the room at the Stonewall a cute, blond, male pool player smiles invitingly—how far will things go? But by now three gin and tonics are knocking on my bladder. Lingering longer would mean a trip to the men's room, and I don't know if I'm that ready to commit.

How to Be a Great Guy
(from *The Politics and Practices of F2M Cross-dressing*)

DIANE TORR

As a man I have access to the world of privilege. I can speak
slowly, as each word, each jewel that I utter has thousands of
years of philosophy behind it. When I pause to reflect, you
imagine that I am contemplating these thousands of years of
philosophy and that I have something important to say. I actually don't need to speak at all. I can simply return your
gaze in a nonplussed fashion.

You, as a woman, might ask me a question, but I have no
need to answer you. I can grunt. I can look away. I can seem
vaguely interested. I don't really need to say anything at all.
I can just look at you with an air of bemused tolerance, waiting for you to say something that might interest me.

When I walk into a room, I am accorded significance
without even opening my mouth or doing anything. If I enter
into a conversation between two women, I am immediately
given attention—no matter that I have nothing of any inter-

est to say on the topic of their discussion. They give me a sense that my opinion is important. They treat me with respect and uphold a sense of my superior knowledge.

Ever noticed how much women smile? That makes them very appealing, because they are unthreatening. As a man, I smile only when there is a reason to smile. When you smile, it's an act of friendliness that could be conceived as conceding ground—thus making you vulnerable to exploitation. As a man, I am given credibility, and people listen to my point of view with concentration. I am expected to be arrogant and forceful because, as a man in a man's world, *I am right.* Hey—even if I'm not, I'd never admit it. Who would go around saying, "Sorry," all the time? I'm not apologizing for nothing. They're lucky to have me around to talk to.

You know, when I was a young guy, I used to think posture was important. You know—chest out, shoulders back, all that crap. I thought it would make me look big—important, you know. Now I realize it don't make any difference what I do; people treat me with the same respect. So I just let it hang—I have a beer gut—I let it hang out. Hey—if you have rounded shoulders, let them hang. People feel sorry for you. They think you have the cares of the world on your shoulders, that you're some kind of Atlas.

Hey, hey. Feel good about yourself, as a guy. What's there to worry about? You've got them by the balls.

PHOTO: ANNIE SPRINKLE

BEEBAN KIDRON

I would prove mine was bigger than Newt Gingrich's, sit down with my legs akimbo, scratch my balls, and pee in a public place. Frankly, I'd be happy when the day was over!

The Fun Dick

M A R Y   M A C K E Y

Acme Novelty Organs, Inc.
212 W. Sycamore St.
Cleveland, OH 46209

Dear Acme Novelty Organs,

Thank you for allowing me to participate in your twenty-four-hour "Cock-Around-the-Clock" promotional. I am returning the Fun Dick in the postage-paid mailer you so generously provided, wrapped in its original packaging as per your instructions. You will note that I have taken the liberty of adding a small pillow and a miniature bottle of bourbon. When I finished with the Fun Dick, he was so worn out that I could not in good conscience send him halfway across the country without providing him with the same amenities enjoyed by those who fly first class.

I have to admit that the depleted state of the Fun Dick is

mostly my fault. Although I hasten to reassure you that I did not break him or even damage him in any way (and am thus not subject to the damage penalty as stated in Paragraph 21b of the Fun Dick Contract), I did spend about four hours romping with him in a variety of pleasant positions that left him in a state that can only be described as complete collapse.

I must say I was surprised that he gave out so soon, particularly since I scrupulously followed the directions in the "Home Entertainment" section of the Fun Dick Instruction Manual. Unfortunately, due to some sort of printer's error, most of the instructions were in Korean, a language I do not, alas, read, but I had thought the diagrams—which were labeled in garbled but decipherable English—self-explanatory until I tried the "Double Pretzel Twish" (as the manual so coyly put it).

Fortunately, the contractor who has been remodeling my house for the better part of the last two years had left a Phillips-head screwdriver and one of his wrenches behind, so with a bit of quick thinking I was able to spare both the Fun Dick and myself what otherwise could have been a most embarrassing trip to the emergency room of the local Kaiser Hospital. But (no pun intended) for a while there it was really "touch and go."

After four hours of "Home Entertainment" with the Fun Dick, I found myself in a state somewhat analogous to that of a Thanksgiving guest who has immoderately dined on the whole turkey, two bowls of mashed potatoes, three tureens of gravy, and six pumpkin pies. In short (or perhaps I should say "in long," ha, ha), I was at that point so satisfied a cus-

tomer that as I lay in bed gazing limply up at my Fun Dick
(who hovered over me, still wearing his cunning little black
leather chaps), I thought about forgoing Christmas shopping
entirely this year and simply giving Fun Dicks to all my
friends.

However, I still had twenty hours left before I had to decide whether to return my dick, so I roused myself with
smelling salts and half a dozen cups of black coffee, then located the (now slightly sodden) Fun Dick Instruction Manual and paged through it. To my delight, I discovered that
"Home Entertainment" was the only section written in Korean. Although subsequent sections were not entirely in
English, I could make out the French, Portuguese, Russian,
and Greek bits without much trouble, and the Aramaic and
Tagalog words were more or less clear from context.

Glancing at Section 2 ("Make War at Home in Your
Spare Time"), I learned that ownership of a Fun Dick entitled me to "start wars; engage in internal, civil, international,
and ethnic conflicts; kill, burn, maim, mutilate, loot, rape,
and pillage; construct biological and/or chemical weapons;
create and deploy hydrogen and neutron bombs; kill small,
large, and medium-sized children; bring on nuclear winter;
and send the human species the way of the dodo bird."

Frankly, this sort of thing isn't my idea of fun. Also, I must
say that I resented the sexism implicit in the idea that one
must possess a Fun Dick or any other kind of dick to do all
of the above, with the possible exception of rape. I have
known a considerable number of dick-bearing individuals
who have no talent at all for mass slaughter, and over the
years I have served on boards and committees with any num-

ber of women who could easily have given Caligula a run for
his money.

On the other hand, I must admit that I found Section 3
("Secrets of Hitler's Vegetarian Cutlets"), briefly tempting.
In the first place, I had no idea Hitler was a vegetarian, and
I found the idea of using the Fun Dick to whip up the egg
whites and sour cream for his "Mock Hasenpfeffer of the
Übermensch" interesting. I was also intrigued by the idea
that ownership of my own personal Fun Dick was guaran-
teed to give me a "95 percent better chance of successfully
setting [myself] up as dictator, tyrant, demagogue, or presi-
dent for life," but, given the domestic competition at present,
I suspect that I would have to relocate to a foreign country to
successfully pursue a career of tyranny, so I decided (regret-
fully) to pass on this one.

Section 4 ("Pick Up Beefcake in Bars") seemed a bit
dated. In my (not inconsiderable) experience, it is still much
easier for someone without a dick (i.e., a woman) to get
"laid" (as the manual so quaintly put it), if getting "laid" is
all one wants. I really doubt that the Fun Dick is going to
"instantly turn [me] into one of the world's foremost stud-
bunnies" (your words, not mine), and frankly I found your
list of "Fifty Foolproof Pickup Lines" embarrassing. What
man in his right mind is going to go home with a strange
woman who introduces herself with the phrase "I got seven
inches of red-hot chorizo down here for ya, honey"?

I think Acme Novelty Organs needs to face the fact that
the Fun Dick, like all dicks, is best used for fun. Take a good
look at your own product: a well-constructed dick isn't a
knife, a gun, a missile, or a passport to instant nooky. It's a

cute, bald-headed, smooth, firm, well-padded pleasure device (with a practical reproductive option), safer than a vibrator—since it isn't likely to electrocute you if you use it in the bathtub—and much more entertaining than daytime television, particularly if it happens to be attached to someone with an IQ higher than a gerbil's.

Given that the Fun Dick simply doesn't live up to its glossy promo, I've decided to return it for a full refund (as specified in Paragraph 46c). Give me Harvey Keitel's love handles any time.

Very truly yours,
Mary Mackey

P.S. I notice that you are having a special on a new product called the Kenneth Branagh Ultra-Tongue (which you are advertising, somewhat infelicitously, by promising that "Emma's Loss Can Be Your Gain!"). Could you please send me a price list and brochure?

Look No Hands/One Night Stand

DOROTHY PORTER

Just for tonight
   my hands don't matter
just for tonight
   I'm no lesbian
just for tonight
   my hands work for me

no longer
   a nourishing girl
      all wholemeal fingers

no longer
   playing ache to get

tonight
   I'm a hot man
      not scared of the dark

tonight
  I'm a reef shark
    cruising the coral park

I won't touch
  won't touch

I'll watch
  my own moving
    piston self

my hands
  still
my hands
  miraculously relaxed

or just flickering
  on the bones of my hips

one hand may stray
  across the back
    of the strange neck
      bent over my axe

or maybe not

because tonight
  my hands don't matter

because tonight
  my hands work for me.

JENNY HOLZER

Many thanks for thinking to invite me. I am flattered to be asked, but I don't want a dick even for one day.

An Evening at the Royalton

CATHERINE TEXIER

I have a dick.

Don't get me wrong; I'm no Neanderthal driven by the bulge in my Calvins and boasting how I can get it up anytime, anywhere. In fact, I am a woman and I love it. I love the plumpness of my breasts and the curve of my waist swelling out to a lush pair of hips and buttocks. I love the sinuous lines, the softness of my tissues, not buff, not tight with well-worked-out muscles, but fleshy, a skin that gives, that takes you in. Actually, up until last night, I loved the hollow between my thighs, shadowy and bushy, a crucible for simmering female smells and humors. I loved to touch it, play with it; I loved to have it filled to the brim.

But now, suddenly, I have a dick, which has seemingly grown overnight, undeniably and stubbornly. It's rock-hard, throbbing, right now, right this minute, in my hand, rising up, defying the law of gravity, swelling to the skies, demand-

ing its due. I have already jacked off twice since I woke up.
I'm sorry, I couldn't help it. My wrist is sore, the muscles in
my right arm tense and crampy, much worse than any cramp
I ever got working at my own womanly attribute. Once more,
I can't resist. My hand migrates between my legs. I touch
myself, grab hold, and get myself off, watching the cum shoot
out, creaming my breasts, running down in thick, pearla-
ceous rivulets, gathering in a little pool around my belly but-
ton.

I am due in an hour at a meeting uptown; I have already
picked my outfit—Armani jacket, gray-blue-lavender tweed
the color of fading heather, and loose pants to give me room
to grow. And a pair of two-tone brogues.

There's a picture I once saw in a porn magazine. A picture of a blond woman, her hair in a flip, a penis curling out
from under her flimsy camisole, talking on the phone.
Laughing. Casual. Nothing to it. Like it was the most natural thing in the world.

What was she, a hermaphrodite? A transsexual?

What am I? What happened to me? I dare not think
about it.

I weigh my nuts in my left hand. They seem to have grown
straight out of my vulva. Is that possible? They're sprouted
with coarse hair, the skin loose, the color of a prickly pear. I
can't help exploring the area with my fingers, searching for
an opening, for the all-too-familiar inviting wetness. But the
lips are now sealed shut. My sex is all exposed to the air now,
feeling the breezes blowing around, my organ both threatening and vulnerable.

I don't like it, I don't like it at all. What's it doing? Dripping at the mouth. I may have to swaddle it, bandage it into a jockstrap, like a lactating breast leaking unwelcome milk, or stuff it into one of my tightest bikinis, the one in stretch black lace from La Perla.

You think that waking up with a dick, you turn into a man? What if you did? What's a man, anyway?

There's no time for philosophical questions. I get up. Got to get going.

As I knew I would, I pass the miniskirts, the tights, the leggings, the high-heeled boots, and head for the Armani jacket, a loose tie on my white shirt, the pleated trousers, the two-tone shoes, a newsboy cap screwed sideways. No drag queen for me today. I look in the mirror. I like the duplicity, the double ambiguity.

⚭

It was a violent night of vivid nightmares involving floods and decapitations. A porcelain doll with mangy blond hair and a red taffeta dress was bleeding between the legs, her mouth open in a silent scream. Doll dreams, I was once told, are symbolic. Symbolic of what, I don't know.

The bleeding was alarming, and even in the twilight of my dream I threw my hands down to check if perhaps my period had started, soaking the mattress. And there it was, plump and snub-nosed, resting in the folds of its foreskin. My heart started to beat violently as I fondled the little bugger, hoping against hope that it was a nightmare. But it responded to my touch immediately, poking its head straight up at attention, and getting frisky, stretching, coming up for air. Expanding in my hand until I could barely close it. My God, it was one of *those*, a baseball bat of a dick!

I watch it, amazed. It's a fucking sausage. And no frankfurter, either! Standing up of its own accord and throbbing. A real woody. It would be the envy of every man I've known or slept with.

My first thought had been to jump into my clothes and rush off to the emergency room at Bellevue, but I had to pee, and when I felt the golden rush spewing froth in the toilet bowl in great warm gushes, I thought better of it.

⚘

They say boy fetuses start as girls, that the clitoris is a vestige of a penis, that in men the vulva is atrophied, the folds swelling into the scrotum, the penis sprouting out from between the folds, soft and snaillike in repose.

Maybe what I am is a late-blooming hermaphrodite.

⚘

I strut around with a secret. A secret weapon; I don't know. How much does the whole apparatus weigh: one pound— two, maybe, when engorged with blood? I would say it's like having an extra breast hanging between your legs. Not a lot of weight added, but it throws off the balance of the body. It changes the focus. Lowers the center of gravity. I've heard pregnancy does that, too: the weight shifts downward. It grounds you. I need to open my legs to accommodate my new bulk. Just a notch, and my hips, in turn, roll with a new swagger and my shoulders follow. Rolling aft and astern. I practice my new gait. I like it. I like what I see reflected in storefront windows.

🍃

The meeting is a piece of cake. It really is. I am a copywriter in an advertising agency and we are hammering out a fetching campaign for a new line of cosmetics derived from all-natural products, like chamomile and snake oil. Everybody in the boardroom is female; everybody from the agency, everybody from the client company. I sit among them, one of the girls, poised to pitch my two lines that are going to change the future of cosmetics advertising; when my turn comes, I'm leaning forward to make a point to the client's second-in-command, a perky redhead with pale green eyes and milky skin and a pair of knockers I used to think made her look like a cow. Her name is Mary. From this angle my eyes find her cleavage, and I dive right in, I notice the edge of a pristine white camisole poking from between the lapels of her jacket. I feel my cock stir and push against the taut lace of my panties. I am amazed. I am torn between touching myself and the urge to insert my hand in the camisole, pop one of her breasts out, and suck on it. Horrified, I reel back and drop my voice, forcefully winding down the presentation and making a case for my two lines—and winning the account.

"Let's celebrate," Mary says, her pretty hands closing her thick folder. "A drink, tonight, at the Royalton, everyone."

🍃

I hesitate. Miniskirt? Pants? It's like being a two-headed monster. Who shall I be tonight? A man or a woman? And do I still have the choice? Once again I opt for the man, as if my new appendage takes precedence over my old pair of breasts. As if this new "thang" is the defining element in my identity. I even stop on my way home to buy myself a smashing Isaac Mizrahi pantsuit for the occasion. Black, tailored; and again the Irish wool newsboy cap. And a pair of heavy black Freelance boots.

"I love your new style," my boss says as I roll into the bar and take the best seat at the table, commanding a perfect view of the Royalton lobby. "I love women who wear man-tailored clothes. I find that incredibly sexy. Garbo; Dietrich; ah, the ambiguity!"

"If you can carry it," redhead Mary says, herself decked out in a silver lamé super-miniskirt and a deep scoop-neck sweater displaying her chest to great advantage. I feel electric vibes floating around the table. I order a Laphroaig, straight up. I don't like the taste of it when it comes, suspect it of being a Johnnie Walker Red Label, or, worse, a Dewar's. I send it back. When the second drink comes, tasting vaguely better, I knock it back and immediately order another.

I am a man. But not quite all man. I am wearing a pair of boxer shorts—flowered, in extra-fine cotton—for ease of motion, and the alcohol and the vision of Mary's white skin bulging invitingly in the deep décolletage combine to stir me in my pants. This time I think of a rattlesnake uncoiling.

Mary is telling a funny story about an ex-boyfriend, something slightly raunchy, and she and my boss giggle with little throaty laughs, their cheeks shiny. Instead of joining in, I watch them. I watch the soft skin of their necks, their small hands, the pure whiteness of Mary's forearms, an almost invisible down softening their outline. I stare at Mary's lips, at her lipstick fading, the mascara smudging the lines around her eyes.

"Ariana, are you all right?"

It startles me. That name. Ariana, my name. Ariana, the pretty blond with the wisps of hair floating around her face, tonight pulled back in a chignon, stuffed under the newsboy cap. Ariana; where are you, Ariana? I summon her back. I pull out my makeup pouch, the Chanel lipstick in its black-and-gold case, the little hand mirror. I purse my lips, redden them until they look flush, glossy, a luscious fruit; I feel ridiculous, outrageously campy.

Mary pulls a cigarette from my pack of Marlboro Lights. Leans forward toward the match I have struck for her (is it the male gene kicking in, turning me into a gentleman?). I cup my hands around the flame, protecting the tip of the cigarette until it glows, waiting for her eyes to thank me, which they do. Her eyes swim a little. They are huge and shiny, two pale jewels. They seem to be overflowing with something humid, as if they are full of fluids. I have seen this look somewhere before, up close. It was on the Greek island of Mykonos, in a tavern, drinking retsina late at night with a group of Germans. The look was in the eyes of a Valkyrie with hennaed hair, and freckles on her nose, and it was directed at my boyfriend, who had the same look in *his* eyes. Half an hour later, they left together and I heard them moaning and banging in her hotel room, which happened to be conveniently located just above ours.

But tonight, Mary's hungry look is directed at me, and

inside my pants something is growing wild, and I long to touch the white skin on her wrist and stick my hand into the black scoop neck of her top. But I let the moment pass. I order another scotch.

My boss says: "I didn't know you held your liquor so well, Ariana. I didn't know you drank at all, actually."

She yawns, gets up. "Look, guys. I'm pooped. We have a big day tomorrow."

She kisses both of us good night on the lips. *Smack. Smack.*

"Tomorrow, nine o'clock in the office, Ariana, right?"

I snicker. "Yeah. Right."

Sleep tight.

After she leaves, Mary takes another cigarette from my pack.

Her lips curl around the little plume of smoke, pushing it upward. We both watch it dissolve into the air.

She looks at me again.

"Have you ever slept with a woman?"

That startles me, gets my heart beating. I can feel myself alive down in my boxers.

"Why are you asking?"

She shrugs.

"Just asking."

I don't mind passing for a daughter of Sappho. We could sneak into the ladies' room and kiss by the water fountain, the one that looks like marble and bubbles gently, sort of like a Roman bath.

But exposing my new manhood? What would that be like?

She puts her hand on mine. She looks determined, desire seeping out of every one of her pores.

"Want to get a room?"

What am I going to say? "You got it wrong, it's not what you think, babe?"

I let her run her fingers between mine, a delicious feeling. I turn my hand palm up, exposing the underside.

I imagine Mary leaning over me, unbuttoning my pants and discovering my dick standing up on its hind legs, stretching to its full height, for the moon. I imagine her aghast, screaming, running out of the bedroom pressing her scoop-neck sweater to her naked breasts. . . .

Or Mary opening her legs wide for me and simultaneously fondling my tits and dick, groaning with delight, her secret dream come true, an overabundance of riches. Like triple layer chocolate truffle cake dripping with hot chocolate fudge.

I look her straight in the eyes. "You don't know what you're getting into," I tell her.

"Oh, but I do," she coos, dropping her hand straight into my crotch.

Liberty

MATTHEW MARTIN

NOTES ON CONTRIBUTORS

KIM ADDONIZIO's fiction has appeared in *Chelsea, Frighten the Horses, Gettysburg Review,* and other publications. Her book *Jimmy & Rita* will be released by BOA Editions in 1997, and she recently completed a collection of stories, *In the Box Called Pleasure.*

ISADORA ALMAN is a licensed California relationship counselor and diplomate of the American Board of Sexology who has for the past twelve years written the "Ask Isadora" column for the *San Francisco Bay Guardian,* the *Advocate* papers in Connecticut and Massachusetts, *Philadelphia City Paper,* and many other alternative news weeklies. She has published two collections of her columns, *Let's Talk Sex* and *Ask Isadora,* as well as the novel *Sex Information, May I Help You?* "Ask Isadora" is now on the Net (www.askisadora.com).

INEZ BARANAY was born in Italy of Hungarian parents and has lived most of her life in Sydney, Australia. She is the author of the novel *The Edge of Bali* and the nonfiction work *Rascal Rain: A Year in Papua New Guinea* (Harper-Collins), as well as other novels and short prose. She currently divides her time between New York and Torres Strait Island, off the north coast of Australia.

JENNIFER BLOWDRYER (aka Jennifer Megan Baring-Gould Waters) has five chapbooks and two proper books out so far. The third book is in limbo, between the publisher and an alleged printer. She's read and sung at many places, from London to Baltimore, and currently teaches a class at Mary-mount Manhattan College.

SARAH BOXER is a writer and cartoonist in New York.

PAT CALIFIA's fiction and nonfiction address the boundaries between pleasure and pain, coercion and consent, and genders of all sorts. She is working on *Sex Changes*, a historical analysis of the development of transgendered identities and communities, forthcoming from Cleis Press.

AVA CHIN lives in Brooklyn and has contributed stories to *The Village Voice*, *Time Out New York*, and *A. Magazine*. Her poetry has been published in *A Gathering of Tribes* and *Excurses*.

KAZ COOKE is an Australian humorist who writes newspaper columns and books and draws cartoons. She is the inventor of the cartoon character Hermoine the Modern Girl and the author of *Real Gorgeous: The Truth About Body and Beauty* (W. W. Norton).

JANICE EIDUS is a two-time winner of the O. Henry Prize. Her most recent book of stories is *The Celibacy Club*. She is also the author of the acclaimed novels *Urban Bliss* and *Faithful Rebecca*, and the short-story collection *Vito Loves Geraldine*. Among the many anthologies in which her stories appear are *Mondo James Dean*, *Mondo Elvis*, and *Growing Up Female*.

AVA GERBER is a Brooklyn-based artist whose work has been exhibited in New York, London, Paris, and Denmark. In 1995 she spent time in Japan on an Asian Cultural Council Fellowship as part of the ARCUS Project.

KERRY GREENWOOD is an Australian novelist and lawyer who lives with a registered wizard and five cats. She is best known for her Phryne Fisher detective novels, including *Death By Misadventure* and *Flying Too High* (Penguin), and the Delphic Women books set in ancient Greece, including *Cassandra* and *Electra* (Reed). She is currently working on her ninth Phryne Fisher novel, *The Eastern Market Murder;* a book of essays on female murderers called *The Thing She Loves;* and the third in her Delphic Women series, *Medea*.

VICKI HENDRICKS is the author of the contemporary *noir* novel *Miami Purity* (Pantheon, 1995). She lives on a sailboat in south Florida with her cat and ferret, and teaches English and creative writing at Broward Community College.

LISA HILL teaches classical political economy at the Australian National University.

AMY JENKINS's fine-art video installations, drawings, and photography explore the notions of privacy, desire, humor, and pain inherent in sexuality. She is a Brooklyn-based artist and has been exhibited and published internationally.

GINU KAMANI was born in Bombay and moved with her family to the United States, at the age of fourteen. She is the author of *Junglee Girl*, a collection of short stories (Aunt Lute Books, 1995). Her short story "Skin Diving in Bombay" is included in the anthology *On a Bed of Rice: An Asian Erotic Feast* (Anchor, 1995), and new work is to be published in *Herotica*. She lives in northern California, where she is working on a novel.

YAEL KANAREK is a New York–based artist and Web designer who has exhibited at the Drawing Center and Momenta Art in New York, and at Elizabeth Valleix in Paris. She is currently engaged in a multidisciplinary project, *Love Letters from the World of Awe*. Kanarek is also the designer of the *Dick for a Day* website (http://www.razorfish.com/d4ad).

GRETEL KILLEEN writes and performs comedy for radio, television, film, and stage. She is the author of six books, the owner of three mortgages, the mother of two children, and the ex-wife of one man.

LYN LIFSHIN has published many collections of poems, including *Black Apples*, *Kiss the Skin Off*, *Blue Tattoo*, and *Marilyn Monroe*. She has edited four anthologies of women's writing, and publishes widely in magazines from *Rolling Stone* and *Ms.* to *American Scholar* and *Chicago Review*. She is the subject of a documentary film, *Not Made of Glass*.

CATHARINE LUMBY is a widely published journalist and art critic. Her first book, *Bad Girls: The Media, Sex and Feminism in the 90s*, is being published by Allen and Unwin. Until she was five, Ms. Lumby thought everyone had his or her own unique set of genitals.

BELINDA LUSCOMBE is a writer for *Time* magazine.

MARY MACKEY is the author of four collections of poetry and eight novels, including the first two volumes of *The Earthsong Trilogy: The Year the Horses Came* and *The Horses at the Gate* (HarperSanFrancisco). Her novels have sold over a million copies and have been translated into eleven languages. She is currently working on the third volume of the trilogy.

MATTHEW MARTIN is an illustrator and cartoonist living in New York City. He draws regularly for *The New York Times*'s op-ed page, and his work has appeared in

Newsweek, Rolling Stone, The New Republic, Harper's, Elle, Esquire, and many other magazines.

BARBARA O'DAIR is a New York–based journalist and poet whose work has appeared in *Mudfish, Semiotexte, Fiction International, The Feminist Review, The Village Voice,* and *Rolling Stone,* among other publications. She is coeditor of *Caught Looking: Feminism, Pornography and Censorship.* HANNAH ALDERFER and MARYBETH NELSON have collaborated on a series of design projects including *Caught Looking; WAC Women Ignite Houston; No More Nice Girls;* and the Public Space and the New American City competition. RACHAEL CARRON is an Irish writer living in New York; she has performed innumerable dull tasks for money.

LANDI OLSEN is a pentapod third-gendered monster. LANCE's (http://www.uidaho.edu/~lolsen/) third and fourth novels, *Burnt* and *Time Famine,* appeared in 1996. The author or editor of nine other books of fiction and criticism, he teaches at the University of Idaho. ANDI's (http://www.uidaho.edu/~lolsen/andi.html) assemblages and collages have appeared in galleries and journals across the country, most recently in Seattle, Portland (Oregon), and Los Angeles. LANDI lives on a farm in northern Idaho.

DOROTHY PORTER is an award-winning poet, writer of adolescent fiction, and songwriter. Of her eight books, the most recent is *The Monkey's Mask* (Arcade), a lesbian detective romance in verse. She lives in Melbourne, Australia, where she is working on a new verse novel.

VICTORIA ROBERTS is a cartoonist based in New York City; her work appears in *The New Yorker*, *The New York Times*, and *The Boston Globe*. Her book, *Cattitudes*, was published by Villard in 1995.

LINDA GRAY SEXTON is the author of four novels and two works of nonfiction, including *Searching for Mercy Street: My Journey Back to My Mother, Anne Sexton*. She lives on the West Coast with her husband and sons, and is currently working on a new novel.

SENATOR SIN is the little-known representative of the submerged feminine voice, who has been recording her experiences faithfully in her unpublished diary ever since her mother first said to her: "You're a woman now." This is the first time she has shared any of her true-life writing with the general public.

AMRUTA SLEE's journalism has appeared in *The New York Times*, *Harper's Bazaar*, *The Sunday Times* (London), and *Elle*. Her work has also appeared in the anthologies *To Be Real* (Anchor, 1995) and *Double X: A User's Guide* (Chronicle, 1997).

JANYCE STEFAN-COLE is a painter and writer of fiction. A native New Yorker, she has traveled extensively and has lived in Mexico and elsewhere. Her stories "Key West," "The Way Home," and "Waking Up in Paris" have all appeared in *Caprice*. She is currently working on a collection of short stories.

CATHERINE TEXIER was born and raised in France and now lives in New York City. Her first novel, *Chloé l'Atlantique*, was written in French and published in Paris. She has also written two novels in English, *Love Me Tender* and *Panic Blood*. Her work has been translated into nine languages. She is coeditor, with Joel Rose, of the literary magazine *Between C and D*, and has coedited several anthologies of short fiction, also with Rose. She has just completed a new novel.

DIANE TORR has been performing in various male personae for over fifteen years, in films such as Abigail Child's *Mayhem* and stage performances by Sally Silvers and Bruce Andrews, as well as Martha Wison's all-woman art band, Disband. She lives in New York, where she conducts workshops and creates her own performance works.

LUISA VALENZUELA was born in Buenos Aires, where she now lives. Translations of her work include *Strange Things Happen Here*, *Other Weapons*, *Bedside Manners*, and the prizewinning novel *The Lizard's Tail*.

TRICIA WARDEN has written two books, *Brainlift* and *Attack God Inside*, both published by 2.13.61 Publications. Her work has also been published in *Purr*, *Bust*, *Oculus*, and *Longshot*. She is currently working on her third book, *Death Is Hereditary*. Warden is also the singer and lyricist with the band Klot.

SARAH B. WEIR is a writer and editor who lives in New York City with her dog, Rex. She is currently working on

Double X: A User's Guide (Chronicle, 1997), a road map to feminism in the '90s.

MARGARET WERTHEIM has written extensively about science and technology for magazines, television, and radio. Her book *Pythagoras' Trousers: God, Physics, and the Gender Wars* (Times Books, 1995) is a history of the relationships among physics, religion, and women. She is working on her next book, *The Pearly Gates of Cyberspace* (W. W. Norton).

For the past six years, CAROL WOLPER has worked as a Hollywood screenwriter, most notably on Simpson-Bruckheimer productions. In 1990 she cowrote *Dirty Dreams*, a "Hollywood" novel (New American Library/Penguin USA). Her magazine credits include *Premiere, Mirabella, Vanity Fair, Buzz, In Style, HG, LA Style* (where she was editor-at-large), and *Los Angeles* magazine, for which she wrote a regular column. She is now working on a feature film for Twentieth Century–Fox and on a nonfiction book entitled *Dining, Dating and Dodging Bullets in L.A.*

JANE YOLEN is known as "America's Hans Christian Andersen" for her many fairy tales. She has written more than 150 books for children, four novels, five collections of short stories, and one book of poems for adults. She is also a wife, mother, grandmother, and a popular oral storyteller.

Made in the USA
Middletown, DE
13 February 2024